Genealogy

As Pastime And

Profession

By
DONALD LINES JACOBUS

Second Edition Revised

With An Introduction By
MILTON RUBINCAM, F.A.S.G., F.N.G.S., F.G.S.P.

GENEALOGICAL PUBLISHING CO., INC.
BALTIMORE   1978

First Edition
New Haven, Connecticut
1930

Second Edition Revised
Genealogical Publishing Co., Inc.
Baltimore, 1968, 1971, 1978

Library of Congress Catalogue Card Number 68-22955
International Standard Book Number 0-8063-0188-0

Made in the United States of America

INTRODUCTION

By Milton Rubincam

Past President, The American Society of Genealogists
Past President, The National Genealogical Society

During the past thirty years there have been published hundreds of books and articles which explain the principles of genealogical research, describe the types of source material, discuss the evaluation of evidence, and demonstrate the sheer fun one gets out of tracing one's ancestors. Many books are excellent, among them Gilbert H. Doane's Searching for Your Ancestors: The How and Why of Genealogy (1937, and later editions),, Archibald F. Bennett's A Guide for Genealogical Research (1951) and Advanced Genealogical Research (1959), Derek Harland's A Basic Course in Genealogy, volume II, Research Procedure and Evaluation of Evidence (1958), and The American Society of Genealogists' Genealogical Research: Methods and Sources (1960, and later reprintings).

But the classic of all time is Genealogy as Pastime and Profession, published by Donald Lines Jacobus in 1930, when there were few books to tell us how to go about this complicated business of tracing one's ancestors. It was written by a man who has complete mastery of his subject. He considered genealogy in all of its phases --- the use of source materials, the evaluation of evidence, the cultural and sociological aspects, the origin of the American colonists, conditions in the genealogical profession, and the compilation of a family history. Many case histories were cited to illustrate the points he was making. In spite of all the "how to do it" books that have been published since 1930, Genealogy as Pastime and Profession tops them all.

F. M. Stenton once wrote that the late Dr. J. Horace Round's "insistence on the importance of family history gave a new value to genealogical studies, and it is probable that no other scholar has made so many or such valuable contributions to his subject". This appraisal of the work of the late great English genealogist and medievalist may be applied with equal truth to his American counterpart, Donald Lines Jacobus.

In the late nineteenth and early twentieth centuries the United States produced some genealogists of the first rank, such as the New Englanders, Colonel Joseph Lemuel Chester and Henry F. Waters, and the Pennsylvanian, Gilbert Cope. But the true "father" of scientific genealogy in this country is Donald Lines Jacobus. In an article in which he paid tribute to one of his colleagues (1960) he described "a new school" of genealogists which began to form about thirty years earlier. "Driven by a zeal to rescue their favorite avocation from its deplorable and desperate state," he wrote, "they started writing and publishing. They wrote accounts of specific families, documented and referenced; they showed by example how problems should be solved, what sources should be used, and how records should be interpreted; they attacked many of the absurdities and atrocities committed in the name of genealogy by the armchair dilettantes who conjured lines of descent from their own fervid imaginations working upon the poorest printed sources."

Mr. Jacobus modestly refrained from mentioning that he himself was the founder of this modern American school of critical genealogists. In 1922 he started a periodical entitled The New Haven Genealogical Magazine. Ten years later his task of publishing the genealogies of New Haven families was completed, the magazine's scope was enlarged, and the name changed to The American Genealogist. Through the medium of his journal he encouraged young authors to publish articles that attacked careless and sloppy research and writing. He built up a Corps of Contributing Editors who assisted him in issuing a magazine that served as the model for all other genealogical periodicals. He led them in tearing down false and fraudulent pedigrees, and in establishing the evidence upon which accurate pedigrees could be based. The early issues of The American Genealogist contain many "how to do it" articles, most of them by Mr. Jacobus, which are valuable lessons in methods of genealogical research. His book reviews were always fair in their appraisal of the genealogies that came to his attention; his criticisms were just and written in kindly fashion. At the time of his retirement as Editor-in-Chief in 1965, when he turned over the editorial responsibilities to one of his associates, TAG, as it is affectionately called by his friends, had long been the leading magazine in our field.

Mr. Jacobus is the author of numerous family histories, all of them models of genealogical research, and of many articles in The New England Historical and Genealogical Register, the National Genealogical Society Quarterly, and other periodicals. He was one of the earliest Fellows of The American Society of Genealogists, an Honor Society limited by its Constitution to fifty members chosen on the basis of the significance of their contributions to genealogy. He is the only person selected for inclusion in Who's Who in America solely on the basis of his achievements as a genealogist.

Genealogy as Pastime and Profession has long been out of print. The Genealogical Publishing Company is making an important contribution to genealogical literature by issuing a revised edition. Its message is timeless.

CONTENTS

PREFACE TO REVISED EDITION

In 1930, one of my busiest years, I was seized with an irresistible impulse to write a book about genealogy. Not a text-book, but a readable introduction to the subject, explaining the fascination it holds for so many of its devotees, touching on some of its cultural aspects, providing some helpful information, and warning amateurs and beginning professionals against some of the pitfalls certain to be encountered.

The book was started one week-end in July of that year. The work was continued every evening of the following week and the book was completed the next week-end. I can still recall sitting before my typewriter one of the hottest evenings of that summer, in my "office" on the top floor under an over-heated roof, clad only in jockey shorts, and with an electric fan playing on me, pecking out a chapter in two-fingered style, with the thermometer registering ninety-five degrees.

Perhaps it was partly because the book was turned out at white heat that it was so enthusiastically welcomed by a group of younger genealogists dedicated, like myself, to the improvement of genealogical standards. The small edition was sold out. Since then, there have been many requests for the book which could not be supplied. It is still suggested as "recommended reading" in some of the lecture courses now given in genealogical method. The late Dr. Arthur Adams, long president of the American Society of Genealogists, in his introduction to the text-book issued by the Society in 1960, most kindly referred to the book as "that classic of genealogical literature."

Because of continuing demand for copies, a decision was finally reached to publish a new edition. A complete revision was required, because some of the statements in the book had become "dated." Conditions in the profession have vastly improved since the book was written, an improvement which I like to believe was encouraged in a small way by the book itself. Besides numerous small changes, one chapter has been omitted, another completely rewritten, and two chapters have been added to provide useful information.

D. L. J.

August 13, 1967

ACKNOWLEDGMENT

The chapters here entitled Genealogical Byways, Early Nomenclature, and Growth of a Colonial Family, and a few paragraphs in the chapter called Puritan Peccadilloes, are reprinted, with slight revision, from articles contributed by Mr. Jacobus to The New England Historical and Genealogical Register, Vol. 77, pp. 10-16, pp. 89-94, and Vol. 78, pp. 154-159, to which acknowledgment is made.

I

WHY THIS BOOK?

The study of one's family history has become the avocation of thousands of Americans. The interest itself is not of recent development, but is inherent in human nature. The most primitive peoples make much of the ties of kin. The Bible is full of genealogies. The aristocracy of every age and land have recognized the importance of keeping a record of their pedigrees. In our own democratic land, it is proper that the interest should not be limited to families of special distinction – in fact, one may doubt whether such a thing as a family of special distinction in all its branches and ramifications can be found; whereas every family is able to boast individual members of unusual merit or attainments. Genealogy has become in America truly democratic.

At the very least, tracing one's ancestry is a fascinating pastime. There are so many ancestors in each successive generation, and the proper spaces for them on the chart or in the record book, and with many it becomes a sort of game to ascertain and fill in the correct names and dates.

Others find pleasure in tracing the connection of their ancestors with historic events, and their contribution, whether large or small, to the founding and early struggles of the American Colonies, and to the establishment of the American nation. Hence the study has its cultural side, often awaking in the student various historical or sociological interests. The first chapters of the present volume will go somewhat fully into the cultural aspects of the study, and the attempt will be made to dissipate a few of the mistaken notions which are often entertained by novices in genealogical research.

Perhaps those who trace their own ancestry unaided derive the greatest amount of pleasure and profit from it. As they become more proficient in criticising and analyzing the information derived from printed sources, they discover that often it is contradictory and untrustworthy. They learn that if they wish to make sure of their facts, the only way to do so is to seek out the primary sources of genealogical information and dig in the original archives. Large numbers live at too great a distance from the homes of their ancestors to make possible a personal search of original record sources. Others lack the time to acquire the special knowledge which this type of research demands. Hence arises the need for a professional genealogist.

The later chapters of this volume will discuss, frankly and honestly, conditions in the genealogical profession; will advise those who desire to enter the profession; will explain what sort of data may be obtained from printed and original sources, giving "case histories" to show how genealogical problems are solved; and will suggest how family histories should be written. Special topics will also be discussed, such as royal ancestry, in which, despite the democratization of genealogy, so many Americans seem to be interested; and the relations between genealogy and genetics and between genealogy and the law.

There is no book, to the writer's knowledge, which attempts thus to treat of all phases of the ancestor cult in America. Although many of the opinions expressed are shared, to the writer's positive knowledge, by many professional genealogists, the writer does not assume to speak for the profession as a whole, and should be understood as giving utterance to his personal views. This volume is not intended as a text-book; nevertheless, it is believed that all who take an interest in the subject will find some of the chapters intriguing, even should they chance to disagree violently with some of the writer's opinions; and novices, whether amateur or professional, will be almost certain to find helpful suggestions and, it is hoped, information of value.

II

PURITAN PECCADILLOES

O God, beneath Thy guiding hand,
Our exiled fathers crossed the sea;
And when they trod the wintry strand,
With prayer and psalm they worshipped Thee.
—Leonard Bacon.

Our forefathers sought the wilderness, and overcame it; but the wilderness, in surrendering, entered into them, and became a part of them; and we are the heirs and the victims of that conquest and its consequences.
—Lesley Mason.

One of the chief delights of genealogical research is the insight it gives us into the motives, the customs, the daily manner of life, of people who lived in a different epoch. For close as our colonial ancestors are to us in generation sequence, and though removed but two or three centuries in time, they lived in a different world from our own. We cannot hope to do more in a short chapter than to tease the reader with hints of the sort of thing he may stumble on if he once acquires the interest to begin digging in the archives for himself.

It has been said that the Puritans were deficient in humor. The Puritan of the old English story who named his dog Moreover after the dog in the Scriptures ("and moreover the dog came and licked his sores") displayed an almost incredible literalness; the story may be apocryphal. But it is true that wit, like gaiety, was not encouraged. The youth who, after rescuing his cow from a bog, told her to go her way and sin no more, was fined for his blasphemous misuse of Holy Writ. Yet it must not be supposed that the Puritans were entirely without a spark of fun. The trouble is that we do not see them in their playful moments. It is only when some prank is carried too far and the practical joker summoned into court, that the documents record anything of this nature. The story of Foote's negro is a case in point. Nathaniel Foote of Branford, Conn., one Sabbath morning, bribed his negro to seat himself in the pew of Mr. Maltby, a wealthy merchant.

It is not difficult to picture the scene. The meeting house is already well filled. Mr. Maltby, waiting for the service to begin, sits in his pew, which because of his social position is close to the pulpit. A tall, full-blooded African stalks solemnly up the central aisle, where members of his race are not permitted. All eyes are focused on him as he unsmilingly progresses towards the front of the house. The hushed expectancy is broken by scarcely audible murmurs of horror as he calmly seats himself beside Mr. Maltby. Boys titter in the gallery. Everyone in the house realizes the humor of the situation. Only the force of habit restrains the congregation from the wildest disorder. Then Mr. Maltby angrily rises and motions the negro out of his pew. The burly fellow hesitates, gets to his feet, and, unruffled amidst the commotion he has caused, retreats down the aisle to his customary place. And the sequel? Inquiries, of course, are made after the service, and the negro, because of his ignorance, is absolved of blame. The real culprit, Nathaniel Foote, is summoned to appear before the magistrates, and is fined for an action which, in the words of the record, was contrary to religion and a profanation of the Sabbath. It may be hoped that he did not regret his little joke, but considered it worth the amount of his fine.

The austere seriousness of the genuine Puritan later degenerated into mere morbidity. Demoniacal angels, reminiscent of the worst Etruscan atrocities, grimace from the borders of the old gravestones. The majority of the epitaphs are of the "prepare for death and follow me" variety. Occasionally there is a quaint frankness, a queer twist of thought, that is worthy of preservation.

The epitaph of Dr. Isaac Bartholomew who died in 1750, today barely decipherable, is traditionally ascribed to his wife. It reads:

> "He that was sweet to mi repose
> Hath now become a stink unto mi nose.
> This is said of me:
> So it shall be said of thee."

Evidently the wife addresses her deceased husband in the first two lines, and he replies in the last two. Or read the cryptic epitaph of Cyrus Hotchkiss:

> "Cyrus tho' pleasant in his day
> Was sudden seas'd and sent away."

Or that of Milly Gaylord, a five-year-old child:

> "Soon ripe; soon rotten.
> Soon dead, but not forgotten."

The epitaph of a young bride reads:

> "The saddest sight in all creation:
> A wedding turn'd to lamentation,
> A mourning groom in desperation."

These epitaphs I can vouch for; the following was sent me by a friend:

> "Here lies the Mother of eight:
> She might have had more, but now it's too late."

The sense of humor has been defined as an appreciation of what is, and what is not, congruous. Can anything be more incongruous than these lines, used as an epitaph for a Connecticut youth who died on Long Island about 1781:

> "Thoughtless he wandered from his native shore
> And laid his ashes in a hostile land."

Those who view graveyards as gloomy places to be avoided can never experience the mingling of reverence and exultation felt by the genealogical enthusiast when at last he stands in front of the long-sought gravestone of a remote ancestor. Nor can they know the furtive delight of collecting curious epitaphs.

Witchcraft in colonial times, and the "Salem Delusion," are subjects which possess a fascination for many historical students, and are another evidence of Puritan literalness. But those who take a perverse satisfaction in writing of our "witch-burning" ancestors would do well to pursue their historical studies a little further; for witches were not burned in the American Colonies. The usual method of execution was to turn them off ladders, leaving them dangling by a rope noosed about the neck.

Saul was not the first to seek aid of infernal agencies when he paid his famed visit to Endor; nor will those who today crowd the offices of astrologers and soothsayers be the last. Belief in witchcraft antedates written history, and in some form still influences the lives of millions. The Puritan had reason to believe in the reality of witches. His Bible admonished him to permit no witch to live. In his day, witchcraft was considered a crime in all the enlightened countries of Europe, where often supposed witches were much more cruelly dealt with than in America. Religion and law alike impelled him to believe, and to act on his belief.

It has become the custom to deride our witch-haunted ancestors as the fanatical victims of an absurd delusion. It is manifestly unfair to condemn them and their contemporaries for failure to view witchcraft in the light of modern psychology. Every age is guilty of absurdities. What of the organized wholesale murder called war? Or the unscientific treatment of the insane and the vicious? Let us make sure that we ourselves do not live in glass houses, before we hurl rocks at those of our ancestors.

The explanation of the witchcraft craze is very simple. Witchcraft existed two or three centuries ago solely because people believed it existed. An angry woman might give a neighbor a hateful glance or utter a half-veiled threat. It would be remembered, and misfortunes subsequently occurring would often be connected with it in the mind of the neighbor. Significance would be extracted out of mere coincidences, and entirely natural events would be attributed to the malignant agency of the suspected woman.

These suspicions would be bandied about, in whispers or even openly. Oftentimes, imaginative children or neurotic adolescents, overhearing the talk, would discuss the matter between themselves. There was a thrill in it, and they would shudder deliciously when the suspected witch passed by them or spoke to them.

Sometimes susceptible youths of either sex became obsessed with the notion that the witch was persecuting them. They would, while tormented with such a delusion, see apparitions of the witch, wraiths created by their own overactive brains. In all this, their parents would see their previous suspicions confirmed. Formal complaint would be lodged against the witch. The afflicted children would be examined by the magistrates, a proceeding which had the unfortunate effect of magnifying their importance in their own eyes and of augmenting the aberrations of such of the children as in reality were afflicted by abnormal or subnormal mentality.

Thus, usually without deliberate malice on the part of any person, the suspected witch might be brought to trial. It must be borne in mind that many of the accused were women of unconventional personality or of temperamental peculiarities which occasioned the suspicion in the first instance. Some were of superior mentality and had ideas which were too advanced for the minds of their contemporaries. Others were of diseased mentality. Probably the extreme fear caused by examination, trial, or conviction, destroyed what little mental balance some possessed. This no doubt explains why a number of witches freely confessed their league with the devil and the evil deeds they had performed by preternatural means.

Very few witches would have been executed in New England if conviction had fallen only on those who confessed or who had been seen in their own persons performing supernatural feats. These were the two kinds of evidence sufficient for conviction, in the opinion of the best judicial minds of that period. Unfortunately, those who presided at the trials in Massachusetts were satisfied to accept the evidence of apparitions of the accused upon the attestation of supposedly credible and reputable witnesses. The Salem craze reached the dimensions of mob hysteria, and many innocent victims suffered.

Search for stigmata on the bodies of accused witches was a relic of the ancient superstitious belief that the devil could have carnal relations with women but could not do so without leaving a mark. Since witches were as superstitious as their accusers, they sometimes underwent the water test at their own request, in the belief it would prove them innocent. In several cases sworn testimony exists that a witch cast into the water bound hand and foot swam "like a cork." The water test was not highly regarded by portions of the clergy and magistracy.

It should never be forgotten that truly religious people were no more common in 1630 than they are today. To read the family histories, one would suppose that the founder of every American family crossed the Atlantic because of high religious convictions, to secure freedom to worship God in the way his conscience dictated. Many motives brought our ancestors to these shores. Religion was one of them, but it was only one of several. Modern scholars place greater stress on economic motives. The landless Englishman could here become a landed proprietor and leave an estate to his offspring. This must have been a great inducement, since a great majority of the emigrants were of the small propertied class. Great hardships the first comers did indeed endure; as great as those endured by soldiers in modern warfare who step back into the primitive from the hearths of comfortable homes. The common people in England three hundred years ago did not have what we would consider comfortable homes; and save only for danger from the native Americans, after permanent homes had been established here they were often as well off as in their former homes in England. If well-to-do settlers missed luxuries they had known abroad, those of the poorer class could not have mourned

for comforts they had never known.

Conditions here were crude, and manners and speech were often coarse. Yet the English language was used in conversation, not differing very greatly from that heard today. If you, intelligent reader, think this is a very obvious and unnecessary statement, have you ever read American historical noves, and do you recall the language used in the conversations? An historical novel of the year 1930 makes its Eighteenth Century characters talk thus:

"Know, then, that this is a private match between two very noted marksmen who are such rivals that I think they would very gladly use one another as targets in a duel. E'en last night at the tavern, and they in their cups, I think it might have come to blows, but the squire, who is a rare wag at times, and hath ideas one would never suspect is so thick a noodle. bethought him of this."

The words are English, but the language is not. No human being in the history of the world ever talked that language. It is a literary fiction intended merely to convey the impression that the person speaking lived some 200 years ago. Eighteenth century writers affected a somewhat stilted literary style at times; they had to show off their education. But their conversation was as free and easy as ours, and they usually employed the inelegant "you was" in place of "you were".

Americans in the Eighteenth Century did not say "hath" unless they lisped; and "bethink" was an archaism which was used only jocularly or in inflated prose writing. There was rhetoric, to be sure; high-sounding phrases are found in the Declaration of Independence and in Patrick Henry's most famous speech. But the common speech of the common man, aside from new words and a few gradual changes inherent in the use of language, was not notably different from what it is today.

Some of our modern story writers who like to write of the earlier periods of our history do, praise heaven, put plain English speech into the mouths of their characters. The rest still cling to that romantic tradition which insists that our heroic ancestors must use a vocabulary drawn from the King James version of the Bible, combined with the archaisms of Spenser in the "Faery Queen" and the artificialities of the worst imitators of Alexander Pope. There are good writers among them, when they write naturally; why do some cling to an absurd convention which should have been laughed out of the novels years ago? These writers would gain much by going to the court records of the period they wish to write about, and reading the testimony of witnesses, which is as close as we can get to the actual speech of people who lived two or three centuries ago.

If they cannot conveniently do that, they can find diaries of the proper period in print; and there is a study in contrast which I should like to suggest. Read first Milton's Areopagitica, his splendid defense of the freedom of the press. Despite a slightly exaggerated style, a relic of the Euphuistic tradition, it is a noble prose with ringing cadences. Then read the Autobiography of Milton's younger contemporary and amanuensis, Thomas Ellwood, written in plain, straightforward English. Whole paragraphs could be quoted from it which, if one did not know differently, might have been written yes-

terday. Ellwood was a Quaker, but aside from the "thee" of his sect, spoke the language of the common people, the language which our progenitors brought with them from England; and he wrote much as he must have talked, without straining for literary effect.

When Paradise Lost was published in 1667, Dryden is reported to have said of its author: "This man cuts us all out." Could anything be more modern?

In fact, the more we delve into the authentic records of the past, the more we are impressed with resemblances rather than with differences. The differences were almost entirely in external conditions; but the people of colonial days were human beings who thought, felt, and acted like ourselves; and they spoke the English language.

III

FAMILY PRIDE

Love covers a multitude of sins.—Paul.

Whatever folly men commit, be their shortcomings or their vices what they may, let us exercise forbearance; remembering that when these faults appear in others it is our follies and vices that we behold. They are the shortcomings of humanity, to which we belong; whose faults, one and all, we share.— Schopenhauer.

The first chapter of the Gospel of Matthew professes to set forth in forty-two generations the descent of Jesus from Abraham. Like most Asiatic pedigrees, it is concerned with the male line of descent, to the neglect of the spindle side. Nevertheless, four of the wives in the pedigree are singled out for mention. Surprisingly, the good old matriarchs, Sarah and Rebecca and Leah, are passed over in silence. The four honored by mention are Tamar, who "played the harlot" with Judah; Rahab, who not only had been a harlot but, what was nearly as bad in the eyes of the Jews, was a gentile by birth; Ruth, who was also a gentile; and Bathsheba, who committed adultery with King David.

The ancestry of Jesus was not impeccable, and the biographer Matthew even went out of his way to specify the descent from four women who, judged by the canons of the time, were of dubious repute. It ill becomes us lesser mortals, then, to insist that our own ancestry should exhibit none but perfect characters. Yet such is human vanity that most of us, when we begin to "shinny up" the family tree, have our eyes fixed on the luscious fruit of Governors, noted clergymen, or military heroes. It is disconcerting to our pride if we find we have picked a wormy apple.

A genealogist told me sixty years ago of a client who bragged that she was sixth cousin of a Governor, and had the relationship charted in her pedigree book, but had never heard of her second cousin in the poorhouse.

There is no need to worry if we find that an ancestor here or there was a shady character. Biologists tell us that if our parents and grandparents were reasonably decent people, so far as heredity is concerned we need not worry about the deviations from rectitude of more remote ancestors. Nature prefers the straight line of normality or mediocrity, and with new blood brought in by successive marriages in each generation, the tendency is always to lower the upcurve of genius or to raise the downcurve of degenerative traits, and thus to bring both back closer to the norm.

Today an adult of early colonial descent on all lines may have ten or more generations behind him in this country, involving a thousand or so individual ancestors. It is unreasonable to suppose that all of this large number will prove to have been superior in character and ability.

Stand on the busiest corner of New York City and detain the first 500 people who pass either on foot or in any variety of vehicle. Line them up and look them over. Say that they roughly correspond, person for person, with each of our first American ancestors, and we shall not be far wrong. There will be, most likely, a very few of exceptional ability, and a very few scoundrels; the great majority will be passably good citizens, mediocre and commonplace. If it be objected that many of those hypothetically drawn into our net on the metropolitan corner may be foreigners, the obvious reply is, that every single one of our first colonial ancestors was a foreigner.

Family pride may be the motive that first attracts us to genealogical studies. If we progress far enough, this pride is bound to suffer one or more jolts when we discover that we had ancestors with whom, belike, we ourselves would not care to associate intimately. Then, if we retain our interest despite our wounded pride, and persevere in our genealogical studies, the time comes when we view these matters in better perspective and we discover that we have gained something in cultural experience.

One of the hardest problems that a professional genealogist has to solve, is the attitude he should take when he finds that wormy apple in a client's family tree. A mere murder can be passed over in silence; if an ancestor was hanged, the date of death can be given without specifying the cause. Doubtless it is wiser, from a mercenary point of view, to withhold unpalatable facts from a client, where this can be done without falsifying records. A family history published in 1961 does indeed state correctly the date and place of death of a member of the family, but without revealing that under an assumed name he was the greatest mass murderer known to American criminal history, or that he was executed on the date specified.

But let us suppose that the problem given to the genealogist to solve is the parentage of one Jane Robinson, born about 1720. After diligent search in the record sources of the proper time and place, the genealogist, from a careful piecing together of evidence from court, probate, and church records, proves that Jane was an illegitimate child. He has solved the problem despite the difficulties involved, and as he takes a pardonable pride in his honest, diligent work, his impulse is to crow over his success and report the findings to his client. But will the client be equally pleased with his success? Usually, not.

The genealogist, if conscientious, will not even consider falsifying the facts as the records disclose them. Two courses of action are open to him. He can lie and tell his client that he has failed to solve the problem. Or he can be apologetic and report the truth. There are objections to the first course, quite aside from the genealogist's disinclination to be forced into a lie. The client may conclude that he did not cover the records thoroughly, and in time may engage some other genealogist on the same problem, paying out money needlessly for a mere duplication of work already done.

Only once have I personally withheld results from a client in such circumstances; and although I still feel I was justified in doing so, my lie did not accomplish its object in the end. A client, long since deceased, wanted her maternal line traced. I traced it and in doing so discovered that my client's mother was born out of wedlock. It was quite a romantic story, and the actual grandparents were finally married some forty years after the birth of their child, and only a year or so before the granddaughter, my client, was born. Being the baby of the family, she had been kept in ignorance of the story, and no outsider had chanced to enlighten her. She had married well, and occupied a fine social position. Feeling that it would be cruel to reveal the facts, I gave the grandparents as married, but omitted the damaging date. Twelve years later, she came to me again. She wanted to join a society to which many of her friends belonged, and one of them, who did a little research occasionally for the amusement of it, had told her that it ought to be possible to locate the marriage record of her grandparents. I knew that it <u>was</u> recorded, in the very town where one would naturally expect to find it, only a few miles from where my client lived. It would have been a terrible blow to her to have this discovery made by this friend; women are sometimes "catty" even in the best social circles. So I warned her to drop the matter, and as gently as possible explained why I gave this advice; and thus my amiable lie of a dozen years before was thwarted of its purpose.

Although intemperance in the use of alcoholic beverages was frowned upon as a vice by our colonial forefathers, indulgence which they considered temperate might be considered excessive today. The quantity of grog consumed by a college president at taverns when traveling would paralyze our hardiest contemporary drinkers. The following episode is from an unpublished diary: "Child of J____ S____ died Sept. 24, 1773 — their foolishness in making a great wedding ye* night before. Both got Drunk, ye father & mother. It is supposed they lay on it and Killed it in their drunkenness. A numerous company of weddingers at night, but not but one of ye whole company attended ye funeral. Shame. "

The parents by no means belonged to the lower grades of society, and they had sufficient means to give a big wedding party. After 1800, temperance societies began to flourish. During the early years of that century, the minister of a parish on the coast, the inhabitants of which were largely seafarers, filled the parish burial register with the names of those who fell victims to the demon rum. Within the space of a decade and a half he listed the following causes of death: "hurt in a Tavern and fell down stairs drunk"; "Rum"; "Drunkard"; "a pauper, an old drunkard"; "intoxicated"; "Delirium Tremens" (a youth of 24 years); "dead in a Ditch — Intemperance"; several, merely "Intemperance"; two others, delirium tremens; and two suicides. Small wonder that the printed copy omits nearly a third of the stated

---

* The "y" in this and other words was not a "y" at all, but the relic of an Old English letter corresponding to our diphthong "th"; and it should always be pronounced as "th."

causes of death, or that the present custodian dislikes to have the original record examined. For these unfortunates were members of the good, old families of the village; one of them was daughter-in-law of the former minister. It is not difficult to understand why many of the old church records have disappeared.

Although illegitimate births were fairly common in New England in colonial days, and considerable laxity prevailed among the unmarried youths and maidens, marital infidelity was rare. Nevertheless, divorce was not infrequent, the husband being the usual offender. The most common cause of divorce was desertion by the husband, sometimes accompanied by infidelity on his part; and several instances have been found of the husband leaving his wife and going to a distant town, where he married a second time without the formality of a divorce. Seemingly insoluble genealogical problems sometimes owe their origin to such extra-legal alliances.

Marriage was not a sacrament, but a civil contract, in the eyes of the Puritans, and in the earlier days all of their ceremonies were performed by the civil magistrates. Those unacquainted with Puritan custom may easily draw erroneous deductions from the fact that an ancestor was married by the Governor. People had to be married by the Governor or by one of the lesser magistrates; and erring young couples who were compelled to marry by court order sometimes had the knot tied by the Governor himself, so no special distinction attached to his officiating.

In Revolutionary times, a young husband who was in service failed to return to his family. The statutory period for desertion having passed, the wife secured a divorce, married again, and had a child by the second husband before her first Romeo appeared on the scene again. This Enoch Arden in real life did not care to fade out of the picture. He petitioned the legislature to set aside the divorce, on the ground that he had been prevented from returning sooner to his family by circumstances beyond his control; the divorce was nullified and the remarried wife restored to his arms. One wonders how the second husband felt about it.

Those who have made unwelcome discoveries far up the ancestral tree should study conditions in colonial times. The country was almost entirely rural, and a state of "village morality" prevailed. Diversions were almost non-existent. The daylight hours were devoted by most of the population to strenuous outdoor labor, and there was little to do in the short evenings except read the Bible and such other books as the goodman's slender purse permitted him to buy. Youth demands a little recreation, and even such harmless country games as the young folk brought from England were frowned upon in the earlier days in New England by the Puritan elders as frivolous and likely to lead to immorality.

Courtship was almost the only pastime left to the young people, and that they indulged in it heartily is evidenced by the court records of the period. Illegitimacy was frequent, and occurred more often in a good class of families than it would today. There was little or no knowledge of birth control. In the Eighteenth Century, a custom known as "bundling" was prevalent in some parts of the country. To sit up courting of a winter evening meant burning out candles and the box fitted with candles came to be known as a "sparking box"; or, if the young couple did not mind the dark, at least it entailed the burning of firewood which had been laboriously cut, hauled and stored. Fully clothed except for shoes, the young people found it more economical, and quite as comfortable, to court in the maiden's bed.

This "bundling" perhaps led to no more premarital intercourse than courting in a hammock or in an automobile, and in judging such a custom, due consideration must be given to differences in external conditions. Alas, our colonial ancestors lacked most of the refinements which we have come to associate with civilized existence; they had their all too human weaknesses, but they had also their rugged virtues. They faced the conditions of life as they found them, and the fact that we ourselves exist is all the evidence we need that these ancestors of ours possessed more strength than weakness. But to harp alone on their virtues is to miss the minor strains which we must hear as well if we are to recreate a truly symphonic picture of their lives.

Much that is splendid and inspiring is discovered in ancestral studies. If here I have touched on the less lovely aspects of the science, my purpose has been to console those who have found undesirable ancestors with the reflection that this is the common lot of mankind.

Possibly one of the incidental functions of genealogical study is to chasten family pride, and to make us more conscious of the essential unity of the great human family.

> We are children of splendor and flame,
> Of shuddering, also, and tears.
> Magnificent out of the dust we came,
> And abject from the Spheres.
> —*Watson.*

IV

GENEALOGICAL BYWAYS

O, call back yesterday, bid time return.
                                                                —Shakespeare.

Time is hastening on and we
What our fathers are shall be,—
Shadow-shapes of memory!
Joined to that vast multitude
Where the great are but the good,
And the mind of strength shall prove
Weaker than the heart of love.
                                                                —Whittier.

The chief value of genealogical study lies in the interest it a-
rouses in colonial history and national antiquities, with a consequent
broadening of the student's cultural attainment. The bare statistics
which form the substructure of the science of genealogy are usually
considered dull and uninteresting in themselves; and so indeed they
are, except to those who find a certain enjoyment in piecing them together — the same sort of enjoyment which some find in picture puzzles or chess problems. But occasionally the genealogist discovers
interesting oddities in the statistics or is able to deduce from them
certain conclusions of general interest.

I hope to show that genealogical research is not so dull and uninteresting as many imagine it to be, but that, in addition to providing essential statistics for other sciences, it opens up new vistas to
the genealogist and offers certain "byways" of investigation which
are very interesting and informative.

Consider the subject of longevity. Statisticians assure us that
the average length of life is increasing, but this can be attributed to
the decrease in infant mortality and the prevention of some epidemic
diseases by means of proper hygiene, quarantine, and inoculation.
Hence, although a greater percentage of infants live to twenty, forty,
or sixty years than formerly, it is doubtful if the man of seventy has
a better chance of unusual longevity than he had a hundred or two
hundred years ago. Every genealogist has found cases of individuals
who lived to the century mark of a year or two beyond it, but experienced genealogists have learned to view claims of extreme old age
with suspicion. Insurance actuaries state that no proved case is on
insurance records of a man living beyond 108 years. The present
writer has not found a proved case beyond 105 years.

Most of the instances where 110 or 120 years were alleged prove
on investigation to be fictitious or grossly exaggerated. The novice

in genealogical research sometimes falls into error through ignorance of these facts; the expert is cautious in accepting statements of extreme age, even when found in town records or on gravestones. The compiler of a Davis genealogy, for example, states that a certain Dan David of Oxford, Conn., died in 1822, at the age of 112 years. Investigation shows that this Dan Davis actually died some thirty years earlier, and that it was a younger man of the same name who died in 1822. The error could have been avoided, if the compiler had been aware of the general considerations stated above.

Amateurs in genealogical research, inexperienced in checking chronological possibilities, often fall into error regarding marriageable ages and the age of parents at the birth of children. In Colonial New England marriage was customary between men of 20 to 25 years and women of 18 to 23 years. The earliest ages which the writer recalls were 16 for a man and 12 for a woman, though earlier marriages may possibly be found; but genealogists are slow to credit extremely youthful marriages unless established by indisputable evidence. There is, however, no limit to marriageable age in the declining years of life, and unions, especially between widows and widowers, were common; many a woman became a blushing bride – perhaps so for the third or fourth time – between the ages of 60 and 80.

The possible age of parents at the birth of children is a matter that can be settled more definitely. Amateurs should always subtract the date of birth of the mother from the date of birth of the child, and should question the accuracy of their records if the result makes the mother more than 45 or 46 years old; for, although instances are on record of women who became mothers at 49 or even at over 50, such instances are very rare. It is also wise, when the father of a family was much over 60, to make sure that the children did not really belong to a younger man of the same name. This, however, is merely a precaution, since there is nothing inherently impossible in a man becoming a father at any age.

The most remarkable case on record of children born when the father had reached an advanced age may be found in the British peerage. It is that of two earls of Leicester, father and son, the former of whom petitioned King George III to deal more leniently with the American Colonies, while the latter died in 1909, one hundred and fifty-five years after his father's birth. The first earl, Thomas William Coke (1754-1842), had by his first wife daughters but no son. He contracted a second marriage at the age of 68, and the union was blessed with six children, the youngest born when the father was 81. The eldest son, another Thomas William (1822-1909), second earl of Leicester, was, like his father, twice married, and had in all eighteen children, the youngest born when the father was 71. This youngest son of the second earl was forty-nine years younger than his eldest half-sister, who was already a grandmother when he was born.

Remarkable instances of paternity at an advanced age have been found in New England, but it is doubtful if any of them can surpass the record of the Coke family. The following item, which appeared in a Connecticut journal over a hundred years ago, is probably exaggerated:

Died, of physical exhaustion, Lieut. John ─────, of ───── at the age of 110 years. He left behind him a young widow and three children, the latter all under 10 years of age.

The interval between the births of children in Colonial New England averaged two years; the interval between the first two was often shorter and that between the last two or three longer, but in many families eight or ten children were born — one every two years with unbroken regularity. This is one of the first observations that amateurs make, when they begin to study the records of the past, and it is an important one; for the existence of a gap of four or five years between children suggests the possibility that an unrecorded child may have been born in the interval. When searching for the parentage of some ancestor whose birth is not on record, a clue can sometimes be gained in this way.

The number of children who can be born of a single union is probably greater than the unreflecting would estimate. If a woman marries at 20 and has one child every two years, she would be 44 at the birth of the twelfth, and it is rarely that more than twelve children of a single union are found. But an article in a scientific journal cites the case of a woman who had borne thirty-three children, all of them twins or triplets. A truly remarkable case of fertility and longevity is furnished by the Pond family. Dan Pond (1726-1783), of Northford, Conn., married Mabel Munson (1730-1793); they settled in Poultney, Vt., and had fifteen children, thirteen sons and two daughters. Several of the sons served in the Revolution, one of them dying in service. The other fourteen children all lived to marry, and most of them lived to an advanced age. The sum total of the lives of these fifteen children amounted to more than a thousand years. If any other American woman, through her children, can equal this record, let her share the laurel with Mabel Pond.

Extraordinarily large families can sometimes be found in cases where a widower with children married a woman much younger than himself, but even in such cases there were seldom more than twenty or twenty-two children by both wives.

It is interesting, at a time when the size of families of New England stock has diminished, to note that the fertility of the royal houses of Europe appears to continue unabated. To take a single instance, the Empress Zita, widow of the late Emperor Charles of Austria, was one of a family of twenty-two children, her father, one of the Bourbons of Parma, having been twice married; her own family of children, because of her husband's death, reached an untimely completion at the number of eight.

The subject of inbreeding is one that frequently arouses the interest of the genealogist. Since one's ancestors double in each generation, one need go back only a few centuries to find the total number of ancestors exceeding the total number of people then living in the world. The explanation of the paradox is the duplication of the same ancestors through endogamous marriages. Hence, in a broad sense, we are all inbred; it is merely a question of how close the inbrooding is. Nearly everyone of from eight to ten generations of Colonial ancestry will find, it the complete ancestry is charted, that some of the names are duplicated. A gentleman of the writer's acquaintance stated that he had twenty-four descents from one of the early settlers in New Hampshire. In charting the ancestry of a lady of Connecticut descent, it was discovered that she had as many as eight, ten, and twelve lines going back to several of her immigrant ancestors. Unquestionably, the endogamous marriages in these two instances are much more numerous than is usually the case.

For the purpose of comparison, it may be stated that the children of the late Emperor charles of Austria are descended 1,990 times from Ferdinand and Isabella, the patrons of Columbus; their cousins, children of the Archduke Peter Ferdinand, have 2,032 descents from the same ancestors; while the twins born in 1921 to Frederick Victor, Prince of Hohenzollern, can boast 2,326 descents. * Astounding as these figures are, it is possible, even probable, that the European peasantry which has lived for centuries in the same localities would show almost as much inbreeding, if genealogical records had been kept. The New England colonists rarely inbred as closely as their European cousins have done, and during the last hundred years there has been much intermarriage with unrelated stocks. It therefore seems ridiculous to assert, as some have done, that the New England stock has been injured by inbreeding. **

The genealogical student finds much to interest him in the distribution of the sexes in the old families; for, while some families "ran to boys" and in a few generations were flourishing in numerous branches, others became almost or quite extinct in the male line because of the preponderance of girls. Biologists are not yet agreed as to the causes that determine sex; but the writer has made an interesting test which may shed some light on the question. *** The sex of the first-born child, and also the sex of all the children, of 139 reigning sovereigns was ascertained, and the results are surprising. For, while out of a total of 876 children 467 were male and 409 female, out of the 139 first-born children 95 were male and 44 female.

It will be observed that, if the first-born children are deducted, the remaining children are almost evenly divided as to sex; and this is what is to be expected in ascertaining the sex of any large number of children. But the excess of males among the first-born children is so amazing as to be of real significance. It may safely be assumed that a large majority of the mothers in these cases were extremely desirous that their first-born children should be boys, in order to se-

---

* With a view to making certain studies in heredity, inbreeding, etc., the writer has charted over 30,000 descendants of Ferdinand and Isabella, and the figures given above are based on these charts.

** Compare the thoughtful note of Rufus Stickney Tucker in The New England Historical and Genealogical Register, vol. 75, p. 317.

*** The figures for the test were drawn from the writer's charts of the descendants of Ferdinand and Isabella. For more elaborate statistics, see the writer's article, "Sex Determination in Royalty" in Eugenical News, vol. II, p. 179.

cure the succession to the throne; and it may be asked whether the mental disposition of the mother can be one of the determining causes of the sex of the child.

Instances can be found where for several successive generations there was no surviving son and the line of descent had to go through daughters — where, in other words, a woman who was herself an heiress had only female issue, who in their turn had only female issue, thus establishing a line of heiresses from mother to daughter. The most singular case on record runs through several titled families of Germany and Austria, and ought to be published in toto to preserve it as a genealogical curiosity; but it has no legitimate place in this book. Suffice it to say, that for eight successive generations, upwards of two hundred years, the line of descent was through females, no one of whom had surviving male issue.

The line starts with Elisabeth, Princess of Liechtenstein, born in 1683, wife of Leopold, Duke of Holstein-Wiesenburg, continues through the eldest daughter in each generation, including the first wife of the famous Austrian statesman, Metternich, and concludes with Elisabeth, Princess of Oettingen, born in 1886, wife of Victor, Prince of Hohenlohe-Schillingfurst. The last-named had four daughters and one surviving son who was born in 1920 and married in 1962 and who, if he has issue, will be the first to break the chain of heiresses in 237 years.

It is also curious to note how the members of certain families adopted the same profession for generations; and it is difficult to say whether this is due to inherited inclination or to the influence of environment and training. The noted Hull family of Wallingford and Derby, Conn., produced within six generations, and in the male line, at least seventeen physicians, two generals, one commodore, six captains, three lieutenants, and many others engaged, either permanently or temporarily, in the military and naval professions. Every genealogist has found similar instances, and the curious can find many such cases noted in books and articles treating of eugenics.

The peculiar names with which the Puritans so often endowed their children quickly catch the attention of the genealogical novice, and it delights even the experienced genealogist to discover such odd appellations as Yet-Once Barstow and Godsgift Arnold. The employment of unusual names frequently provides clues towards the elucidation of an ancestral line, but the novice is as likely to be misled as correctly guided by clues of this kind. It sometimes happens that the duplication of the same given names in two families is nothing more than coincidence, and such considerations as locality and social status are almost as important as nomenclature. An exception is the use of surnames for Christian names, which in the first hundred years of New England history usually signified relationship to the family whose surname was used. But after we pass much beyond the year 1750, the employment even of surnames is of doubtful value as a clue to relationship.

Such are some of the genealogical byways into which the feet of the student may stray, whether for pastime or for mental profit. Space is lacking to pursue any one of these byways very far, but enough has been said to indicate whither they lead. Genealogy and chronology have been called the handmaids of history; it is equally true that genealogical statistics are essential to students of eugenics, biometrics, and human heredity. The genealogist not only supplies these essential data to his brother scientists, but finds his own intellectual horizon broadened by straying at times into these cognate fields of science.

V

EARLY NOMENCLATURE

It has often been remarked that the early settlers in New England, particularly those who came in the great wave of immigration between the years 1620 and 1650, were more nearly homogeneous than were the founders of the southern colonies. Certain it is, that such contrasts as existed in the former case were less violent than that, for example, between the aristocrats and the deported criminals of Virginia. Yet, outside of primitive tribes, it may be doubted if an entirely homogeneous people has ever existed; and the Puritans, though mainly sprung from the English yeomanry, had their castes. Difficult as it frequently is to draw the line of demarcation in specific instances, in a general way the first generation of New Englanders may be divided into two classes. The first class, constituting a majority of the population, was composed of those who were in sympathy, at least, with Puritan ideals. The second class, a substantial minority, drew from various elements: the adventurers who hoped to better themselves materially in the New World, the servants who accompanied well-to-do Puritans, the ne'er-do-wells who felt safer outside of England.

The trend of history is often reflected in the very names borne by the men and women who played a part in it. The Assyriologist, for example, merely on the strength of the names borne by certain kings, whether Semitic or not, can reconstruct the probable course of history four or five millenniums ago. It is interesting to see how far the succession of historical movements, the changes in manners and standards, during the first two centuries of New England life, affected the nomenclature of the inhabitants.

The first settlers bore names of three different types, those of English origin, those of Hebrew origin, and those which were intended to have a moral significance. The old English names, on account of their connection with the Church of England, were not in favor with the Puritans; those who bore them were, as a rule, either not Puritans at all or else had been christened before their parents turned Nonconformists. For a hundred years this class of names was not common, since even non-Puritan families were influenced by the prevailing mode. In some instances – though these are comparatively rare – filial piety caused the retention throughout this period of an old family name, such as Roger or Edward; and there was one family which, uninterruptedly for generations, endowed its daughters with the sturdy Saxon name of Æthelred. And despite the prejudice against English names, it is curious to note that this prejudice apparently did not apply to surnames; from the first it was a common practice to give a boy his mother's surname.

The most numerous of the three types of names employed by the Puritans was the Biblical group. Here with the exception of thoroughly Anglicized names, such as John, James, or Thomas, the Old Testament patriarchs and prophets were the favorites. The established church in England had made common use of New Testament names, and the Puritans wished their children to be distinguished from Conformists even by their personal names. The name Peter, because of that apostle's traditional connection with the Papacy, was not common; but it is not so easy to explain the aversion to Paul. This name was as rare as Seraiah, Shebaniah, Bezaleel, or any of the least known Biblical characters. There was a natural dislike of Cain, Delilah, Jezebel, Herod, and the rest of the Scriptural rascals and vampires. Judas is rare, though Jude and Judah occur; we also find Judith, the feminine of this name, indicating an acquaintance with the Apocrypha. Adam and Eve, the parents of all our woe, do not appear to have been popular. Other names, like Christopher and Christian, Angel and Angelina, Michael and Gabriel, though sanctioned by the Anglican Church, were perhaps held too sacred for mortals to bear; they are among the most uncommon names to be found in Puritan families. But the names we meet for generations in every town and hamlet of New England are those of the patriarchs from Abraham to Joseph and his brethren, those of the famous leaders and kings of the Israelites, such as Moses, Joshua, Gideon, Samuel, and David, and those of the Major Prophets.

However rare they may be, it is possible to find namesakes of practically every person mentioned between the covers of the Bible. The chief reason for this is probably the old custom of opening the Bible with the eyes shut and giving the child the name which happened to be nearest to the pointing finger. This custom may explain the occasional use of place names, like Eden and Sinai, instead of personal names. The name Notwithstanding Griswold may be similarly explained. So also the fact that in 1721 one Samuel Pond inflicted on his helpless son the name of Mene Mene Tekel Upharsin. It is not easy to think of any other rational explanation unless Mr. Pond, having in mind the interpretation of the handwriting on the wall, intended to commemorate the final downfall of the Stuarts, which seven years before had been assured by the succession of the House of Hanover. The confusion of the Biblical Mehitabel with the Latin Mabel – the names were used interchangeably – often perplexes the amateur genealogist, and the origin of the confusion is not apparent.

Of course the most interesting, perhaps the most characteristic, names were those signifying moral attributes, intended to incite the bearers of them to lead godly lives. Names of this type in New England were much more common for girls than for boys, and were seldom so grotesque as some of the monstrous combinations employed by the Puritans in England. Among the popular names for girls were Content, Lowly, Mindwell, Obedience, Patience, Silence, Submit, and Temperance. What a commentary on the qualities deemed desirable in woman! Charity, Mercy, and Prudence, in use before Bunyan wrote, received an increase in popularity from their appearance in his allegories; the name Beulah originated with Bunyan. Comfort, Delight,

Faith, Hope, Thankful, Desire! With names like these, how charming – at least in their girlhood – these Puritan damsels must have been. Marriage at an early age, the bearing of eight or more children, and the loss, irreparable to them, of their teeth, aged them rapidly. If they could only have provided themselves with false teeth and grandmotherly spectacles, how few old hags there would have been to suspect of witchcraft.

Among the names given to boys we may note Consider ("let us consider together, saith the Lord"), Ransom ("A ransom for many"), Remember ("Remember now thy Creator in the days of thy youth"), and Saving (referring, not to thrift, but to the grace of God). Virtue and Zealous occur, but are infrequent. It is remarkable how quickly the names of this group were standardized, one portion being assigned to boys, the other to girls. The reasons determining this assignment remain obscure in many instances. Why should Deliverance, Relief, and Recompence customarily be assigned to boys, and Experience, Reliance and Repentance to girls? It is odd that Wait and Waitstill should be masculine, Hope and Hopestill usually feminine, that Lovewell should be a man's name and Freelove a woman's. Elder William Brewster of the Mayflower named a son Love, but elsewhere this name is usually feminine; and a single case has been found where Mercy, a popular name for girls, was applied to a boy. The sex of the rarer names was differently standardized in different localities, and even in case of the common names uniformity was not absolute.

Some names of this group apparently were improvised to commemorate some special occasion. Preserved is an example of this class. During the War of the Revolution many boys were christened Freedom, Liberty, or Independence. The name Doctor was sometimes bestowed on a seventh son in allusion to the superstition that seventh sons possessed an intuitive knowledge of the use of herbs. Mariner was occasionally bestowed on the son of a seafaring family, and there is at least one instance of Sailtrue, not a bad name for a sailor. The relation between parent and child determined such names as Lent, Gift, and Welcome. The names Lament and Trial, sad to say, were considered appropriate for girls born out of wedlock; incidentally boys born out of wedlock were usually given the name of the reputed father. Posthumous girls occasionally were christened Orphana; similarly, the Biblical names Benoni and Benjamin (in remembrance of the death of Rachel) were frequently given to boys whose mothers died in childbirth, while Ichabod was popular for posthumous boys. There were also names peculiar to certain localities. In ancient Woodbury, Conn., for instance, three feminine names, though rare elsewhere, were very common: Emblem, Concurrence (usually abbreviated to Currence), and Olive (a variant of the stately Olivia). Other names were peculiar to certain families: the mother of an early settler in Hartford rejoiced in the Italian name of Violet, which for generations was bequeathed to her descendants; and this name was otherwise so exceedingly rare that, whenever it occurs in this region, the genealogist at once surmises and seeks to establish a connection with this particular family.

Among the more unusual names we must not fail to mention Be-

Fruitful Brockett, who died in infancy, and Maybe Barnes. The origin of the latter name has not been ascertained; possibly it was intended for the surname Mabie. Just why Matthew and Rhoda Blakeslee called their fifteenth child Careful, we shall not attempt to surmise. At times these Puritan parents exhibited a woeful lack of humor or else humor of a tasteless variety. We cannot suppose that the parents of Preserved Fish, Green Plumb, or Ivory Keys (boys), or those of Active Foote, Rhoda Bull, Rhoda Way, or Silence Noyes (girls) intended a double entendre. On the other hand, the father of Happy Sadd must have selected his son's name with deliverate malice, as surely as Jonathan Rose intentionally alluded to the Song of Solomon when he named his son Sharon. Some of the early Puritans undoubtedly cherished the same delight in the bizarre which at a later date (about 1800) caused Dr. Osee Dutton to name his eleventh child Sebastian Maria Ximenes Petruchio and his twelfth child Thomas Albert Buonaparte Jefferson. Polycarpus Nelson of Mamaroneck, N. Y., had his eldest son christened Maher-Shalel-Hash-Baz. How many today are well enough acquainted with the Bible to open its pages to that fearful name?

From about the middle of the eighteenth century onward a gradual change is apparent in the ideas and manner of life of the inhabitants of New England. Contact with the British and French during the Indian wars broke the crust of their provincialism, and the long War of the Revolution, which placed them shoulder to shoulder with the other colonists – the Dutch of New York, the gentlemen of Virginia — could not but broaden their mental horizon. The colleges, which at first had been mere classical schools for the training of clergymen, became more humane; their library shelves held more books of a secular and liberal tendency; college societies began to enact English comedies. As the merchant class grew more affluent, the younger generation studied law and medicine. Culture was imposed on wealth. It was natural that, as the opportunities for sensuous luxury and for intellectual enjoyment increased, there should be a rebellion against the narrowness of Puritan dogma and the aridity of Puritan life. Many were infected with deism, a philosophy to which the poetry of Pope – not to mention the Calvinistic fatalism of Jonathan Edwards – afforded an easy transition; many more embraced the Church of England, which, in addition to its religious and aesthetic appeal, tolerated the more innocent pastimes.

What was true of the upper stratum of New England society was true in even greater measure of the lower strata. The descendants of the adventurers and roisterers who had caused so much annoyance to the early Puritans had only in rare instances risen to position in church or civil life. They were still at the foot of the ladder, still made to feel their inferiority. The Anglican Church was at this time doing missionary work in the Colonies; the Congregational societies in some of the New England Colonies constituted the established church, for a long period acknowledged by the civil government and authorized to tax all citizens, whether members or not, for its maintenance. Eager to gain converts, the Anglican missionaries did not spurn these black sheep of Puritanism, but welcomed them to the fold.

It is not difficult to understand the success of the Church of England in proselyting those who hitherto had been of little standing in New England society. Doubtless the prestige and the more elaborate ritual of the mother church impressed them; here, too, they found a religious body which was more tolerant of frivolity, more ready to admit the weakness of the flesh and to pardon the carnal sins. But the most powerful desire was, perhaps, to improve their social status, to form a community of their own, in which they could move undisturbed by the censure of Puritanical bigotry. Thus it came about that between 1700 and 1775 the newer aristocracy of wealth and the "white trash" of the New England Colonies both gravitated towards the Church of England.

The middle classes, still constituting a vast majority of the population and carrying with them the remnants of the older Puritan aristocracy of birth and personal worth, clung to the tenets of their fathers; but even here the infiltration of new ideas is discernible. Religious zeal lost its intensity and moral fibre its toughness. Manners grew more lax; there was greater freedom of intercourse between the sexes. The eighteenth century was altogether a more comfortable period to live in than the seventeenth century had been. The old standards were breaking up; society was growing more complex; opinions were becoming more divergent and irreconcilable.

Through the transition era, this time of shifting ideas and changing manners, the trend of history may be read in the names bestowed on the children of the age. The Biblical names still greet us, but the uncommon ones begin to drop out until only the more popular survive. Side by side with them the good old English names, long disused, but not forgotten, reappear with increasing frequency. The Church of England was in no small degree responsible for the revival of Saxon names, for the Anglican families had employed these names throughout the period when most of their contemporaries were Israelites indeed. Our gratitude is not lacking as Hachaliah and Zachariah make room for Henry and Edmund, and we hail the return of Dorothy and Margaret. But we must not in our complacency overlook a long list of names of an entirely new class which make their appearance in the registers of births. Where once it had been essential to choose names from one book, the Sacred Scriptures, it now became the fashion to filch names from any book. A renascence of the classics is indicated when we find ourselves confronted with Virgil, Æneas, and Horace. The great English novels of the generation were also read; the popularity of Richardson may be gauged by the number of Clarissas and Pamelas who kept the home fires burning for the soldiers of Valley Forge, nor were Fielding's Amelia or Smollett's Narcissa neglected. Shakespearean heroes and heroines, especially the latter, come into favor: Miranda, Orlando, Silvia, Celia, Julia, and a host of others. Other names, unfamiliar, yet modern in appearance when contrasted with Obadiah and Keturah, were doubtless stolen from some forgotten romance, some "best seller" of that generation. Calvin, Luther, and the names of other theologians and divines become common, and in Lamira the hymnal appears to have furnished at least one name. Finally, a few names, such as George and Frederick, Caroline and Henrietta, were borrowed from royalty and English aristocracy.

In a word, it became at last the unquestioned prerogative of parents to take names from any and every available source; and we must not forget the influence of newspapers in the latter half of the eighteenth century in propagating the names of public characters. But perhaps the most remarkable feature of the nomenclature of the new era was the transformation undergone by the names of the preceding period, nor could any more striking illustration be found of the greater laxity of manners prevailing than in the nicknames which fill the baptismal registers, both Congregational and Episcopal. Among the feminine derivatives of common occurrence were Sally (Sarah), Molly and Polly (Mary), Betty (Elizabeth), Patty (Martha), Nabby (Abigail), Sene (Asenath), Hitty (Mehitabel), Dolly (Dorothy), Sukey (Susan), Tonty (Content), and Bede (Obedience). Though less frequently, masculine names were subjected at times to a similar diminution, as Tom and Ned, Riah (Azariah), and Jere (Jeremiah) bear witness.

We have crossed the threshold of the nineteenth century, a century in which the increasing complexity of social strata, the increasing diversity of interests, and the diversity of blood introduced from Ireland, Germany, and elsewhere are matched by a corresponding diversity in the nomenclature. It will be wise to take our leave of the New England of the Puritans at this point, before the threads of the discourse are quite lost in the labyrinth we are approaching.

VI

ROYAL ANCESTRY

Boast the pure blood of an illustrious race,
In quiet flow from Lucrece to Lucrece:
But by your father's worth if yours you rate,
Count me those only who were good and great.
Go! if your ancient, but ignoble blood
Has crept thro' scoundrels ever since the flood,
Go! and pretend your family is young;
Nor own, your fathers have been fools so long.
What can ennoble sots, or slaves, or cowards?
Alas! not all the blood of all the Howards.

—Pope.

Occasional perusals of the Genealogical Department of the Boston Evening Transcript and other publications have convinced [me] that, in spite of the fact that "all men are created equal" and in spite of the good old American contempt for royalty and the "effete nobility of Europe," the American genealogical public have an exceedingly strong desire to deduce their descent by hook or by crook from the same "effete" royal and noble houses of Europe. Furthermore, an investigation of these claims usually shows that not one in twenty of such pedigrees can stand up under the searching test of modern scientific investigation.

—G. Andrews Moriarty in The New England Register.

Those of us who trace to the American colonials can work back our ancestral lines for eight to twelve generations in this country. Then comes a break. Most of the first settlers came from Great Britain or Holland. A large majority were from England, and in this chapter we shall arbitrarily limit the discussion to those who were from England.

Many are satisfied when they have charted their ancestry to the first "come-overers," but of late years more and more interest has been taken in the earlier English ancestry. Genealogical students now wish to know in what English village their first American ancestor originated, and to carry the line still further back if possible.

English research is a field in itself, and because of the great difference in conditions, a vast amount of special knowledge is needed before the genealogist is equipped to be an expert or specialist in English research. Some employ English genealogists, while others employ Americans who make periodic trips abroad or arrange to have the research done by their correspondents there.

Since a very large percentage of our colonial settlers were of yeoman stock or lower grades of society, it is rather difficult to push most lines back more than three or four generations; for after we get back of the beginning of the parish registers, records of the lower social classes are scanty.

Mr. J. Gardner Bartlett, one of our foremost specialists in English research, wrote: "Of the five thousand heads of families who came between 1620 and 1640, less than 50 or not 1% are known to have belonged to the upper gentry of England, and less than 250 more, or not 5%, can be considered as from the minor mercantile or landed gentry. No peers nor sons of peers, no baronets, nor their sons, but one knight and no sons of knights, were among the founders of New England. "

To which Mr. Ernest Flagg. in his excellent book, The Founding of New England, adds the following comment: "Yet if one were to credit the family genealogies he would conclude that the great majority were of gentle extraction. Sometimes it is only a crest or coat of arms that is claimed, but very often descent from the most prominent English house whose surname is the same or similar to their own; and not a few, in all seriousness, claim royal descent. At the public libraries, books purporting to show such connection for American families are fairly worn out by much handling. "

Among 500 or 1,000 first American ancestors, one can often discover two or three who did come from the English landed gentry. These lines, because of land ownership, can not infrequently be followed back for many generations, occasionally to the period of the Conquest. But it is never safe to accept, as too many American genealogists do, the pedigrees as printed in heralds' visitations and county histories, without independent verification from contemporary documentary sources, many of which are now in print.

It sometimes happened that a county gentleman somewhere up the line married a knight's daughter, and by going back on that line, perhaps one of the knights married an earl's daughter, and once we strike the peerage it is not difficult to acquire some sort of royal ancestry.

Just what advantage there is in claiming a fractional drop of royal blood, is a complete mystery. For every one descent I might claim from King Alfred, I could claim a million from the peasants of his time, if records had been kept of the lower classes. However, if one desires the fun of tracing a long descent, say for thirty generations, it cannot be done unless one succeeds in tapping a royal line; for the farther back we go in the Middle Ages, the scantier the records become until even royalty itself vanishes in the mists of legend.

But if one finds amusement in embarking on this kind of adventure, surely it loses even what little significance it possesses unless care be taken to verify each link in the ancestral chain, for if a single link give way, the royal descent is a mere fiction. The credulity of Americans, even of many American genealogists, in matters of this sort is sad to witness.

A great impulse was given to the claiming of royal lines by the publication of Browning's book, Americans of Royal Descent. Most of the lines given in this book were not proved by any valid sort of evidence, and a large number of them were false and could readily be disproved. The book passed through several subsequent editions, which corrected some of the errors, but Browning still remains one

of the poorest authorities that can be quoted for English ancestry.
However, once a line of this sort is put in print, no amount of honest
criticism can kill it, and although many of these lines have been disproved again and again and the evidence printed, the uninformed still
continue to quote them.

Later, Dr. David Starr Jordan in Your Family Tree dissemin-
ated a large number of royal descents, and while he was not personally
responsible for the pedigrees given, his name in the minds of many
endowed these pedigrees with an authority which they do not merit.
In the main, they are copied from the poorest printed sources that
could have been selected, and are not entitled to credence unless thoroughly verified.

It is not generally understood by American genealogists that
many of the older European books on royalty and peerage have been
superseded by the work of modern scholars in the fields of history
and mediaevalism. Let us first consider the English peerage. The
pioneer worker on the peerage was Dugdale, who went to original
sources for information, but the field was so immense and his facilities so limited, that although his Baronage remains a standard authority, it must be amplified and corrected from the work of modern
scholars. The later peerage writers seldom went to original sources
and uncritically accepted much pleasant fiction furnished by members
of the families treated, together with many honest mistakes.

One peerage writer copied from another, and the result is that
Burke's Peerage, while a good authority for the period from 1700 to
the present, was long a poor authority for the earlier period; and the
latter is precisely the period in which Americans of colonial descent
are interested. Recent editions, however, have discarded many of
the legends and fictions once included. Modern scholars, such as
J. Horace Round in Peerage and Family History and other books and
articles, and other scholars whose findings have been published in
English periodicals such as The Genealogist, have followed Dugdale's
example in going to the contemporary documents, and the result has
been a new, accurate genealogy based on scientific methods of research. Old fictions have been cast into the discard, and many remarkable discoveries made.

Another step in the right direction was the publication of The
Complete Peerage, by G. E. Cockayne. An immensely amplified edition of this work, started under the editorship of Gibbs, is now available, the articles prepared by scholars of repute, and containing information that adds immeasurably to our knowledge of English titled
families in the Middle Ages.

The biographical notices in the great Dictionary of National Bi-
ography are authoritative, though occasionally in need of correction
as the result of research done since its publication. The Dictionary
errs, for one example, in its account of the origin of the House of
Mortimer.

It is not to be expected that American genealogists could, without years of study and training, decipher the records written in a difficult abbreviated form of Latin and in mediaeval French. But they
should at least learn what printed authorities can safely be followed,

and cease quoting old editions of works on the peerage.

When we come to the royal families of continental Europe, American genealogists exhibit an even greater ignorance. Anderson's Royal Genealogies seems to be their favorite source. This monumental work, published in 1732, is still a reasonably good authority for the period from 1400 to 1700, though notably weak in tracing the royal houses of Russia and the Scandinavian countries. For the earlier period it follows all the myths and fictions that Anderson found in print, and although he himself cautioned that some of the lines given were probably not historical, they are still copied out and reprinted by the uninitiate. The book is full of inaccuracies regarding even the historical monarchs of France and Germany, especially during the period from 600 to 1100, and should never be used as an authority for this period.

Many of the European dynasties were founded by able and unscrupulous upstarts. When established on the throne, they, or their successors, were flattered by venal genealogists who fabricated long and noble pedigrees for them. A considerable number of these fictitious lines were accepted by the uncritical genealogical students of a former day, and repeated in many compilations like that of Anderson. Modern scholars have disproved many of these fictions, and have rejected others for lack of proof.

Modern scholarship has been busy on the Continent, and the results of this research are available in French, German, Spanish and other tongues at a few of the larger American libraries. It is my sober opinion that American genealogists should not attempt to handle mediaeval royal genealogy unless they have trained themselves to specialize in this field, and are able to read historical works in several languages. Unless they can do this, the best European authorities are sealed books to them.

In a field where professional genealogists so often show their ineptitude, the amateur is a lost lamb. In fact, amateurs are responsible for many of the erroneous royal lines that have appeared in print; and once they have originated, they have been copied and reprinted by the type of professional incompetent who believes that the printed word can never lie. A few of these fictitious lines which I have had occasion to investigate are mentioned briefly below.

The magnificent history of the Henry Whitney family published by Phoenix in 1878 is marred by the inclusion of a chart purporting to set forth the descent of Henry from the Whitneys of Whitney. Henry's parentage is unknown; the line of descent given is based on two fictitious wills invented by a fraudulent English genealogist and innocently accepted by the compiler.

The long vaunted descent of the Seymour family of Hartford, Conn., from the ducal house of Seymour was based on forged entries in a Bible. The forged character of the printing and writing was quite apparent to any genealogist expert in reading the script of the period; and the research of the late J. Gardner Bartlett in England proved conclusively that the American family originated from yeoman stock.

The Tuttle Family, published in 1883, although the compiler did not profess to know the parentage of the first settler, William Tuttle, nevertheless states that William was the great-great-grandson of a William Tothill and Joan Grafton, and then proceeds to trace a royal line through the Graftons. It has since been proved that the American settler came from a different family in England and did not have this Grafton ancestry.

A little book entitled By the Name of Rice states that the author had searched in England and found that Deacon Edmund Rice of Sudbury, Mass., was great-grandson of a Rhys who married Katharine Howard, daughter of the second Duke of Norfolk. The evidence was not presented, and it was preposterous on the face of it to believe that good old Deacon Rice was so closely related to the premier Dukes of England. On behalf of a client, I had the claim investigated, and the will of Katharine failed to name the son through whom the descent was claimed. The uncritical are still tracing their ancestry back to all the kings in the deck through this fictitious line. *

The history of the Pomeroy family, compiled by an amateur, but containing the results of research in England by a professional, asserted the descent of the American family from the Pomeroys of Berry Pomeroy. The only real piece of evidence for this claim was a photographic reproduction of an English pedigree; but an inspection of the original pedigree showed that the photograph had been "doctored," so that the reproduction contained more data than the original, and precisely the data which was needed to substantiate the claim. The research of Mrs. Elizabeth French Bartlett put a quietus to much grandiloquent ancestry.

The statement has often appeared that the noted Anneke Jans of New Amsterdam was a daughter or granddaughter of William the Silent. Some sixty years ago, a descendant had the royal arms of the House of Orange painted on her coach. This was triply ridiculous. In the first place, the House of Orange did not become royal until several generations later than William the Silent, hence his descendants were not entitled to the royal arms unless members of the royal line. In the second place, William left sons, and no descendants in the female line would be entitled to use his arms; even if he had left no male descendants, the female line would only have been entitled to quarter the arms. Finally, the family of William is well known and a matter of documented history; Anneke could not have descended from him except illegitimately, and in that case could only have used his arms (if at all) with a bend sinister. But not a shred of evidence has ever been presented, so far as I am aware, to back up this absurd claim. It is a queer commentary on human nature that people who would be shocked by illegitimacy in an American forbear should be so eager to believe that an ancestor was a bastard of the Prince of Orange.

Another dubious line is that of another Whitney immigrant, John of Watertown, Mass. Here a great deal of genuine research was done,

---

* Mention of the Rice claim, as well as of the John Whitney claim on a later page, is made by kind permission of Mrs. Horatio Ford of South Euclid, Ohio, on whose behalf research was made by the writer and by Col. Charles E. Banks of Boston, Mass.

and a beautiful book published containing the evidence in full. Unfortunately, the critical link in the pedigree is the identity of Thomas, supposed father of John, with Thomas son of Robert, third son of Sir Robert Whitney. The only evidence for this identity is a pedigree in the British Museum showing the claim of a later London Whitney to be heir male of the Whitneys of Whitney. The claim was not backed by any evidence, and presumably was mistaken or fraudulent, for a careful analysis of available dates shows that the generations in the pedigree would have been incredibly short. If correct, a father and son must each have married at the unusual age of fifteen; and in view of this, the conclusion of the author cannot be accepted without stronger proof than this book presents.

These are examples of the royal lines which have been generally accepted by the uncritical; and some of them, I understand, have been accepted by such societies as the Baronial Order of Runnymede and the Order of the Crown. It would seem that there is scarcely an American family for whom some such claim has not been made. There are a few families for whom royal lines can be proved by sound legal evidence. Many of the false claims are so absurd that it is hard to understand how they can deceive any except those who wish to be deceived. That is one of the saddest features of this subject; the capable and honest genealogist too often receives no gratitude from the client from whom he has taken a cherished illusion. Genealogists know this, and it is not surprising if the less scrupulous ones hesitate to deprive a wealthy client of his minutia of royal blood.

But let not this last wish be vain:
Deceive, deceive me once again.
                    —*Landor.*

VII

GENEALOGY AS A PROFESSION

By their fruits ye shall know them.
—Jesus.

Diligence is the mother of good luck.
—Benjamin Franklin.

Conditions in the genealogical profession are unsatisfactory. Any person, regardless of education, experience or natural ability, can set up to be a professional genealogist. No course of training is required, no examinations as to fitness have to be passed. For this very reason, the profession appeals tó many who lack the mentality for this kind of work, and who might be unsuccessful in other professions.

Those who employ a lawyer know whether or not he wins their case; those who employ a physician can judge whether or not he improves their health. But unless those who employ a genealogist themselves have considerable knowledge of genealogical research, they have absolutely no criterion by which to measure the capacity of the genealogist they employ. If the latter reports success and sends them an ancestral line, they are easy dupes and do not readily discover that the line is inaccurate or is based on unreliable printed sources. Because of this, incompetents can survive longer in the genealogical profession than they could in most.

Retired clergymen, school-teachers who desire less nerve-wracking work, and elderly people who wish to add something to their incomes or pensions, often view genealogy as a genteel profession which fulfills their requirements. Some of these people possess the natural mental qualifications for the work and, after they have gained experience, become capable genealogists. Others lack the type of mentality which research requires and never suspect their own unfitness for the work they are doing. Very few professional genealogists are deliberately fraudulent, but many are so naive or careless or haphazard in their work that the results are fully as bad.

From the monetary point of view, conditions are also unsatisfactory. It must be borne in mind that an established genealogist is under rather heavy expenses. In the first place, there is bound to be a great waste of time due to the large amount of correspondence. Many people write to genealogists without any expectation of employing them or of paying for information, while others write asking whether the genealogist can supply the information they desire without special research. Sometimes a commission results, and in any case both courtesy and business judgment demand that all these letters be answered. If the genealogist assumes this burden personally, it cuts badly into his working time. If he employs a secretary, her salary must be deducted from his gross earnings.

If the genealogist does not live where a large genealogical library is accessible to him, he must try to accumulate a reference library of his own. Even if he resides in a big city, he can save time both for himself and his clients if he owns the books he most frequently needs to consult. Most genealogical books are published in small editions and hence are high-priced at the start; when they are out of print, the price of second-hand copies goes up alarmingly, and it ordinarily requires a large investment of capital for the genealogist to equip himself with the books he needs. Usually his reference library has to be built up by slow stages over the course of several years. However, many of the basic out-of-print genealogical reference works and some of the major works on heraldry have been reproduced by photo-offset by the Genealogical Publishing Company of Baltimore and its affiliate, the Heraldic Book Company. And since these are available at relatively moderate prices, it is now possible to build up a reference collection at a cost that is not prohibitive. Original research involves considerable travel to reach the record sources, and under present conditions a car is essential, and its cost and upkeep are considerable.

Finally, there are many expenses, small in themselves, which in the aggregate foot up to incredible totals. Among these must be classed paper, postage, typewriter, carbon sheets, advertising, and floor space. For as his collection of books, note-books, manuscripts, and letter files increases, he must live in an apartment large enough to house it all.

When all these factors are considered, it is not surprising if the genealogist of national reputation finds at the end of the year that, despite a good gross business, he is no better off financially than some of his less known competitors in smaller towns. At any rate, enough has been said to indicate that genealogy is less lucrative than most professions and many trades.

There is of course another side to the picture. The work is pleasant, it takes the genealogist away on trips to different places, with expenses paid, and it introduces him to a very agreeable class of people. For it has been my experience that a vast majority of the people who employ professional genealogists are pleasant, kind, and interesting individuals. In nearly fifty years of professional experience, I have had only two bad accounts. This of itself speaks volumes for the character of those who employ genealogists.

And then there is the work! If the genealogical bug once bites you, you are a doomed man, and never again will you be happy except when attempting to trace the elusive ancestor. It has all the fascination of a game for one who loves it. It is like working out a chess problem or a cross-word puzzle; but much more exhilarating, for the pawns in this game were once living human beings. You have ancestral charts in blank, which theoretically can be filled in completely with the names of your ancestors; and there is no elation akin to that which you experience when a long-sought forbear is discovered and an empty space on the chart becomes a name and an entity.

Naturally, there is drudgery in every kind of work, and when you are chained to genealogy for ten hours a day, six or seven days a week, it takes problems of more than usual interest to bring back the old thrill. After half a century, however, I can still enjoy that pristine elation, and if one is a born genealogist, he can never bring quite the same zest to any other kind of work.

What qualifications should a professional genealogist possess? First of all, enthusiasm for the work. But he must have more than this, for I have known enthusiastic genealogists, both amateur and professional, who were not even capable of grasping the elements of a problem.

He must have a mind that can grasp and retain and work with an infinite mass of detail. He must be by natural bent a detail worker, not an executive. An unusually good memory is a tremendous asset. If after working an hour on a problem or an ancestral line, the would-be genealogist cannot carry all the essential elements of names and dates in his head without reference to his notes, he would do well to decide that nature intended him for some other profession.

Imagination is another important factor, and I would rather see an inexperienced genealogist show too much imagination than not enough. The unimaginative genealogist works too mechanically; he may cover thoroughly the records that seem essential, but if these fail to yield the desired information, he gives up the quest. The more imaginative searcher may detect clues in the very same records, and by following them up may eventually solve the problem. Of course the imagination of the novice is somewhat wild, and he is too apt to discover clues in every record he sees. Experience usually tones down the too exuberant imagination, and the genealogist needs to develop a critical judgment which will enable him to decide without wasted effort what clues are likely to have significance. Clients prefer not to employ genealogists who run up expense accounts following will-o'-the-wisps without result.

Special knowledge is also very necessary, and the genealogist cannot learn too much of the social customs, laws of inheritance, paths of migration, and much else pertaining to the history and culture of our country during the colonial and early national periods. To make clear the kind of knowledge a genealogist must acquire, let us consider a few examples. If a John Peters is listed in a muster roll of the Revolutionary War, and one man of the name is found who was aged forty-two, and another who was but seventeen, to which would the service most probably pertain? Would it affect the problem whether the service was in the Continental Line or whether it was in the militia?*

Could a John Brown who lived at Springfield, Mass., be appointed an officer of the Northampton militia company (or train band) in 1758? Or could he have captained a company composed mostly of Northamp-

---

* The youth would probably be the soldier, if in the Continental Line. Men older than forty-two often served in the militia companies, which as a rule were only called out to repel attacks. These are probabilities; there are exceptions.

ton men recruited for service in the French and Indian War?

Could a William Rowe whose tombstone states that he died April 23d, 1800, aged eighty-two years and eleven days, be identical with a William Rowe who was baptized on April 6th, 1718?*

If the will of Robert Thompson in Boston in 1668 failed to name any daughter Mary, is it possible that a Mary Thompson who was married in Boston in 1666 was nevertheless his daughter, provided other dates are in harmony with the assumption?**

If Edmund Brown in 1675 sold land at Fairfield, Conn., which had been laid out to Thomas Williams, an original proprietor, and if you fail to find a recorded conveyance from Williams to Brown, would you assume that Brown had married the daughter of Williams? Would it make a difference in your conclusion if Brown's wife signed the deed with him? What would be the interpretation of the wife's signing if the land were located in the Province of New York?

The names used are fictitious, and I have not given answers to all the questions. Let the reader who thinks genealogical research requires no special knowledge or training study these hypothetical questions. They are but a few examples of the wide range of knowledge which the professional genealogist must acquire if he is not to misinterpret the records he finds and mislead his client.

The genealogist must be accurate. Accuracy is a prime essential for the professional. No living person is infallible, and the best of genealogists make mistakes. There are bound to be occasional errors of judgment in interpreting the meaning of records, but errors of this type should be infrequent if a genealogist is experienced. There are clerical errors, usually the product of fatigue, or caused by a momentary mental lapse. In printing, there are overlooked typographical errors; though here we should not be too hasty in blaming the genealogist. Such is the sheer perversity of print that I have known errors to appear in a printed book in places where the final proof was correct. Such errors can only be blamed to some accident in the composing room which occasioned hasty resetting of a few lines. The work of any genealogist should be judged by what is characteristic, not by what is exceptional.

A good test for accuracy is to take a page in any book, and copy it with fair rapidity; then have another person read the page to you, specifying every capital and punctuation mark. If after several trials you still make two or three mistakes to a page, your accuracy is below the standard required for a genealogist. Within limits, accuracy may be improved by training. But some persons possess a photographic vision which others lack, and if the trouble is organic, no amount of training can make you a more accurate copyist.

---

* Yes; the calendar change in 1752 makes it possible.
** Yes. A daughter was often portioned in movables at marriage. If she had received her full portion before her father made his will, he would ordinarily so specify. However, the fathers of the period kept account books as a rule showing what had been advanced to their adult children; and sometimes wills were crudely or informally drawn and failed to mention children who had received their full portions.

To sum up, the professional genealogist should possess certain natural aptitudes, sharpened by experience. He should be painstaking, thorough, and accurate. He should be able to weigh evidence; to assemble in logical order a host of details; to construct hypotheses and test them. He needs the detective instinct, and experience must have taught him which of several clues is most likely to lead him to his object. He needs imagination, toned down by long training, and directed by sound reasoning. Especially he needs an excellent memory. Granted this natural equipment, much study and special knowledge are essential.

A genealogist should not be opinionated, but should always keep an open mind and be ready to admit, on occasion, that his first conclusion was a mistaken one. Those who fear that an admission of error will damage their professional reputations are usually those whose reputations as genealogists will not suffer much from any admission. Adherence to truth is more important than professional pride.

He that can have patience can have what he will.
—Benjamin Franklin.

VIII

TO BECOME A PROFESSIONAL

The ascendant hand is what I feel most strongly; I am bound in and in with my forbears. . . . . We are all nobly born; fortunate those who know it; blessed those who remember.—R. L. Stevenson.

Professions pass for nothing, with the experienced, when connected with a practice that flatly contradicts them.—J. F. Cooper.

Several have sought my advice as to how to become a professional genealogist and I have had to confess that I do not know. The reason is that I have been a genealogist almost from the cradle, so there is little in my personal experience which would be useful to the young man or woman who desires to enter the profession.

For what it is worth, however, here is my own story. When I was about eight, I was given a copy of Dickens' "Child's History of England," which had in the front a genealogical chart of the English kings. My mother was interested in her family and had collected information from older relatives, which she had written down. Children are imitative, and I felt impelled to chart the information she had on our family in the same way that the kings were charted in my history book. Having been raised on the Bible, I remembered the wonderful genealogical lists in the Old Testament, and did not rest satisfied until I had charted all the kings, priests and notables of the early Hebrews. My next discovery was that our old American Cyclopaedia contained accounts of many of the European monarchs, beautifully cross-referenced so that I could work out their relationships and chart them.

My chief worry was one of the King Ferdinands. Perhaps the Cyclopaedia was guilty of an error, or perhaps I misinterpreted one of its statements, but if I understood it correctly then a certain King Ferdinand was his own great-grandfather. I knew a man could not be his own father or grandfather, but I almost strained my childish brain trying to figure out whether he could be his own great-grandfather. The mystery of time began to reveal itself, and I came to realize that dates were as important as names in unraveling a pedigree.

When I was ten, a cousin of my mother's joined a patriotic society, and told us of examining the little old first volume of vital records in the New Haven Registrar's office. I gave my mother no peace until she took me there to see it. After that, I went there by myself. The Tax Collector was our near neighbor and friend, and learning of my interest, he introduced me at the Town Clerk's office and showed me the original first volume of the New Haven Colony records. Thus I learned where the land records were kept, and what a wealth of genealogical material is buried in them. I found my own way into the Probate Court and the Superior Court.

By the time I was fifteen I was able to read the difficult Seventeenth

Century script as readily as modern handwriting, and when I was six-teen I had two genealogical articles accepted, one by the now defunct Connecticut Magazine, the other by the New England Historical and Genealogical Register. While in a preparatory school, a friend at Yale introduced me to the attendants at the Yale Library, and I obtained permission to utilize their fine collection of genealogical books.

My first work was tracing my own family lines, which on my mother's side were mostly from New Haven or vicinity. Some missing lines remained, and in the attempt to locate them I began systematically to trace the rest of the New Haven families. When I was seventeen, I first planned to publish a history of all the New Haven families; but another seventeen years elapsed before I realized this boyish ambition by beginning publication of the New Haven Genealogical Magazine.

My father used to try to discourage me from spending so much time on research, which he felt would jeopardize my future; there was no future in genealogy, he used to tell me, and I never argued the point, for there did not appear to be much of a future in the profession at that time. One of my keenest disappointments is that he died when I was twenty-four, before I had the chance to prove to him that the time spent on research had not been wasted after all.

I had returned to Yale to take up post-graduate work, intending to become a teacher; not that I felt any special leaning towards teaching as a profession, but that the vacation of three months in the summer appealed to me as time I could devote to genealogical research. However, my father's serious illness caused me to decline the first and only teaching position I was offered, and to take over some of his work. At his death, I succeeded him as secretary of a building and loan association, and held this office for several years.

During that period, I continued to work evenings on my compilation of New Haven families, and would often steal a few minutes from my noon lunch hour or after I had closed the office for the day, to run into City Hall and do a little more research. But as the association grew in size and my work there increased, I realized that I could not continue to serve two masters. Although this position offered an assured future, I resigned and made my plans to take up genealogy as my sole means of support. I had been working for clients occasionally since my college days.

Two months after my successor took over the secretaryship, war was declared on Germany. Nothing could have been worse for my plans, for genealogy was a neglected luxury in war days.

Discharged after my return from overseas on the day following my thirty-second birthday, I settled on a little three-acre farm. My plan was to reduce living expenses by keeping chickens, cultivating a kitchen garden, and selling asparagus and other specialties. This was a wise move, for the first year I took in only about a thousand dollars from all sources, – and incidentally, lived within my income. But even so small a farm consumed too much of my time, and livestock, even if only poultry, requires regular attention and feeding, so that, being without a car, I could not get away from the place readily enough to handle all of the research work that offered.

Conditions could scarcely have been worse, so this seemed a propitious time to launch the New Haven Genealogical Magazine and thus make reality of my boyish dream. It cost over two hundred dollars for the subscription circulars and the first issue, and the number of subscribers won was far below my expectation. Although not really successful as a financial venture, this publication nevertheless brought me recognition as a genealogist, and many commissions from clients.

Seeing that the tide had turned, I abandoned my three acres, and eventually settled in the city, more convenient for research. For many years I have had all the work I could handle; and thus ends my personal story.

If it has any moral at all, it is that if you are a born genealogist, you will sometime, somehow, find a way to devote all your time to genealogy.

Unless you have the assurance at the start of good-sized commissions from two or three well-to-do clients, I would not advise trying to wrest a living from genealogy alone. A better plan is to secure, if possible, a part-time position, which will enable you to give the balance of your time to genealogy, until you have made a reputation and can give up the other work.

I have never advertised much, and do not believe it pays to spend much on advertising, but it is probably beneficial to have your "card" in one or two of the best genealogical magazines. As in all professions, your clientele grows chiefly through satisfied clients recommending you to their friends. In the course of a few years, this process gains momentum, and brings you sufficient work.

If you live in a town in the eastern part of the country, a town that has not had a good historian, spend your spare time combing the local records. Arrange systematically the family data you collect. Always take references to volume and page for each item of information, for if some future client seeks information, you will want to be able to give the references without doing the research over again. Remember that other people are interested in genealogy, and in a small town your work will quickly become known. Your local town officials will perhaps be glad to turn over genealogical queries to you and others will send inquiries to you as the local historian and genealogist. In time, some society or wealthy individual may become interested in financing the publication of your genealogical history of the town, if you are unable to finance it yourself; and with a book of this type to your credit, your reputation will be much enhanced.

And how are you, and your family if you have one, to live while you wait for Time to accomplish these wonders for you? Unless you have a small independent income, the suggestion of a part-time position is the best I can offer.

If you live in a western town, my inclination is to say: go east, young man or young woman, or else await your next incarnation to become a genealogist. Roughly speaking, the original record sources for the first tow hundred years of our history are in the east. Western genealogists work under the terrific handicap of having to trust printed sources which so frequently are untrustworthy, or else of having to employ eastern genealogists to search original records. Some cut the dilemma by making periodic trips east and doing their own research here.

Many eastern genealogists are very supercilious in their attitude towards the work of the westerners. I do not share this feeling, for I know western genealogists who are well equipped by nature and training for research and who have excellent work to their credit. Nevertheless, they do work under almost insuperable disadvantages. They can perform a great service to the cause of genealogy by collecting, in their different communities, fast-disappearing Bible records and recollections of aged people, in addition to their local public records, and such collections will grow in value as time passes. Western genealogists are often superior to eastern ones in establishing the connection between the pioneering ancestors and their eastern origin, for they have made more of a study of the tides of emigration to the west.

But when the eastern origin is ascertained, and it becomes necessary to trace the early generations through the colonial period, too many of the western genealogists are satisfied to follow old errors that have been repeated from book to book, instead of undertaking an independent investigation. I can sympathize with them, for most clients set a limit to what they are willing to spend, and a trip east or the employment of a genealogist here would often raise the total cost too high. It is an unfortunate situation, and one for which no remedy appears.

There are, of course, some excellent genealogical libraries in the mid West and far West, so far as printed sources are concerned. But when original research in documentary sources is required, the great library of the Latter-day Saints at Salt Lake City is the only one which has a large amount to offer, for they have microfilmed an immense quantity of original record books, probate and land records, in the eastern states.

For those who reside in the larger cities, there are sometimes other opportunities to establish themselves as professionals. If you are sociable, tactful, and diplomatic, join two or three of the patriotic societies, do a little "handshaking" with the right people, and let the members and officials know that you do genealogical work. When there is a vacancy, one of the societies may elect you to the post of genealogist, which usually, if it does not provide a salary, pays for the checking of application papers. At least this will bring you a steady income, whatever the amount, and more important, people will be impressed by the fact that you hold an official position, and this may result in private commissions.

Some societies have extremely capable genealogists who merit their official positions. Others are unfortunate in having selected incompetents; and as most of the society members have little real knowledge of genealogical methods, the incompetents may succeed in retaining their positions for a considerable length of time. Conditions are improving in this respect, however, and many of the societies are now more critical in choosing their genealogists. The personal factor should not be neglected, though, as sociability and good-fellowship often have an influence, particularly if more than one candidate is in the field.

In conclusion, the following practical suggestions may be of value:

1. Be sure that you have the type of mentality which genealogical research requires, and that you have had sufficient experience, before you decide to become a professional, especially if you will have to derive your livelihood from the work.

2. Write up two or three families you have worked on for your own amusement, and if possible get your accounts published by genealogical magazines. This will give you practice in arranging your scattered notes with formal precision. If an article is published, you will be able to refer to it as an example of your work. Study the method of arrangement generally employed in the periodicals you have in mind, and follow it exactly. If the editors find your material intrinsically valuable, this attention to form may result in early publication, for the simple reason that genealogical magazines are usually under-staffed, and the preference may be given (between two articles equally good) to that article which requires the least editorial labor.

3. Most important – this is a recent development – a Board for Certification of Genealogists has been set up; the address (1966) is 1307 New Hampshire Avenue, N. W., Washington, D. C. 20036. This Board will examine the credentials of genealogists and will issue a "degree" of C. G. (Certified Genealogist) to applicants whom it finds qualified. Those just entering the professional field may perhaps find it helpful to make application to this Board. *

4. Have a personal letter printed, stating your rates, the territory with which you are best acquainted, where you are best qualified to undertake original research, the length of your experience, and requesting the recipient to give you a trial. Send copies to your friends and acquaintances. Send copies also to a few well-established professionals. Do not look for too generous a response, particularly from the professionals. They may not need research in your section the moment your letter arrives.

5. Reports to clients should always be typewritten unless your handwriting is unusually legible. Always make a carbon copy of each report. You should have them in your files for future reference. Arrange the material in logical order with full references. If the problem was a complicated one, it is often well to present first your abstracts of records and then to comment on your deductions from these records. Send a bill with each report, and unless you have been authorized to work up to a monetary limit not yet reached, await the client's reply before continuing the research.

6. In working for another professional, it is generally inadvisable to do so on a basis of exchange. It is simpler and often more satisfactory to charge for your work at the time, and later to pay the other professional if you call on him to work for you. Be particu-

---

* A description of the work of this Board is contained in the Appendix.

larly careful to do precisely what the professional calls for; if you go beyond what he requests, you may be duplicating a part of the work he has already done personally, and he will either have to stand the loss or charge his client more than should have been necessary. It is naturally annoying to a professional if another, to whom he assigned a specific part of the work, attempts to "hog" the entire commission. Inexperienced professionals sometimes make this mistake through ignorance or through a desire to impress the professional employing them with their ability to carry the search through to a conclusion.

7. In reporting failure, always explain just what records you have covered and the conditions which impeded success. Do not send a mass of unrelated genealogical data to soften the failure; this might lead the client to believe that you did not understand what he wanted or that you failed to grasp the problem. Do not recommend a continuation of the search in other directions unless you think the chance of success reasonably good.

8. Give your best advice as to how the search should be conducted; but if the client insists despite your advice on conducting it in some other way, remember that his money, not yours, is paying for the search, and follow his instructions. Then, if the search fails, he cannot blame you. Some clients leave the search entirely to the discretion of the genealogist; others prefer to direct the campaign and to have the genealogist carry out specific instructions.

9. If a client criticises your work or your charges, consider the criticism with an open mind. It is possible that without realizing it you have given some cause for the complaint, and you will not want to make the same mistake a second time. When satisfied that the criticism was unjust, write at length and explain amiably why the work was done in this manner or why your charges had to be such an amount. Most people are reasonable when they understand a matter.

> *God helps them that help themselves.*
> *—Benjamin Franklin.*

IX

COMMERCIAL FIRMS

Half the Truth is often a great Lie.
—Benjamin Franklin.

With the great growth of interest in the subject of ancestry, it is not surprising that some commercial houses were attracted to the field of genealogy as a possible source of profit. The question is pertinent, when does genealogy cease to be a profession and become merely a business?

The genealogist, like any professional man, takes a genuine pride in his work. Anything that he puts in print must be made as accurate as possible, and he would scorn to copy and reprint data from other books without investigation of the reliability of the books used, or if necessary, an independent investigation in original record sources. As with other professional men, there is a personal relation between the genealogist and his client, and he feels a responsibility to give his client nothing but accurate information. He charges a fee for services which his ability, training, and experience enable him to render.

In making this distinction between the professional genealogist and commercial houses, the difference of attitude is the essential thing. The commercial house does not feel the same sense of personal responsibility to the client; the emphasis is on giving the client what he wants, rather than on giving him the truth and nothing but the truth. If professional genealogists are sometimes found to be hostile towards the commercial firms, it is because the latter have lowered genealogical standards and helped to render conditions in the profession even less satisfactory than they were. A client who has employed either an incompetent genealogist or a commercial firm, and who afterwards learns of gross inaccuracies in the data paid for, naturally forms a low opinion of the genealogical profession as a whole.

Most of the commercial organizations that have entered the genealogical field have been publishing houses. Some of these specialized in genealogical printing; and when they did not get enough family histories to publish for compilers of such works, it was natural that they should seek to stimulate business by doing publishing on their own account.

One of the earliest, and incidentally one of the best, of the publishing firms to evolve such a scheme, was Joel Munsell's Sons of Albany, N. Y. By 1900 Munsell's Index to American Genealogies had run through five editions. This is a useful work, though now far out of date in view of all that has been published since 1900. * The pre-

---

* Munsell's Index and the Supplement, 1900 to 1908, have been reprinted by the Genealogical Publishing Company of Baltimore.

sent writer carried on this type of work by publishing three volumes of a genealogical periodical index (up to 1953), * and this work has since been carried on by others.

Munsell's also brought out a series of books under the title, American Ancestry, which sold well and must have been a profitable undertaking. People were invited to send their own family lines for publication, and I believe a charge was made for inclusion, or at least those included subscribed for copies of the book. Of course no publication of this type can claim to be authoritative. It is bound to be unequal in merit, since the material is furnished by a large number of people. Some of this material shows evidence of much research and careful compilation; while some is of a decidedly lower standard. ** These books furnished the prototype for many subsequent publications.

A decade later, a New York City firm was in the field with a somewhat more ambitious scheme. The north Atlantic states were divided into zones, and three or four-volume genealogical histories issued for each zone. Agents approached those who had achieved prominence of any kind in their respective communities and "sold" them the idea of including their family lines in these books. The opportunity was given them also of writing what they pleased about their own careers, and this must have been an excellent selling point, for every man would like to be his own biographer.

These books have had a wide circulation, and are among the first books to be consulted by novices and, I regret to say, by some of the less experienced professional genealogists. Although each set published had an editorial staff, the price charged for inclusion was insufficient to enable the staff to spend much on original research. Much valuable material was printed where the person who furnished it had had research done by experts. But where it had to be left to the editorial staff to furnish the ancestry, there was too much dependence on inferior printed sources, and even on downright guessing.

Another New York house specialized on coats-of-arms, and issued very handsome books for private clients. Very little original research was done, and the genealogical material printed was often untrustworthy. Emphasis was usually placed on noble English families of the same surname, despite the lack of connection with the American family, and rarely was any evidence presented for the right of the American family to use the coat-of-arms which in gorgeous colors faced the reading matter. A competent professional can recognize a book of this type at a glance, and know that he cannot trust the genealogical data in it without independent verification.

All books of this type have some genealogical value and a proper sphere of usefulness. It can usually be taken for granted that the information about present-day descendants, and their parents and grandparents, is correct, and the writer of a family history who is inter-

---

* This three-volume Index to Genealogical Periodicals, originally published in 1932, 1948, and 1953, has been reprinted by the Genealogical Publishing Company of Baltimore.

** This twelve-volume set, originally published from 1887-1898, has been reprinted by the Genealogical Publishing Company of Baltimore.

ested in all of a certain family name, can thus, like Samson, find honey in a lion's skull. The same observation applies to many town and county histories, which often contain biographies and genealogical sketches derived from many sources and too often are not safe to follow so far as the earlier generations are concerned.

A publishing house located in another metropolis evolved a different scheme for drawing dividends from genealogy. Common surnames were selected and books published, one to each surname, purporting to be family histories. The printed census records, printed war rolls, genealogies and town histories, and many other printed works were combed for mention of each surname, and the resulting hodge-podge was called a family history. If these books were labeled "source material from printed authorities" on the Smith, Jones or Robinson family, nobody could criticize adversely a publication of this type; for it does bring together into one volume what can be found in scattered printed sources and make it readily accessible to those living far from the large public libraries. Oftentimes valuable information or clues at least can be found in a book of this type; but it is misleading to call it a family history, for such a book cannot justly lay claim to being either comprehensive or authentic. In 1930 this organization was closed by the Postoffice Department for "false and fraudulent promises."

In Chicago seven volumes were published, the first in 1925, of a work called The Abridged Compendium of American Genealogy. This work belongs to the same genus as American Ancestry mentioned above. It differed from it in being more comprehensive, more condensed, and less lucid in arrangement. It presented the pedigrees of a large number of people on one or more lines from their first American ancestors. Like other publications of similar type, the Compendium was of unequal merit, depending on the source of the matter printed. Some of those who furnished their data had looked up their ancestry with care or employed genealogists to do so. Unquestionably others furnished much less trustworthy data, and where their personal knowledge was slight, the editorial staff supplied the deficiency by using such printed sources as were available. As no references are given, users of the Compendium cannot determine how authentic any specific statement is, and because of the high proportion of known errors, conscientious genealogists do not use statements made in this work without verification. It is often a useful reference work for those who know how to employ it properly and who do not trust its statements too implicitly.*

In 1928 Mr. Frederick Adams Virkus, publisher of the Compendium, organized "The Institute of American Genealogy." Mr. Virkus was himself the director of this organization, and in fact, sole arbiter of its policies, for the Council, which was formed at his invitation, was merely advisory. The Institute inaugurated an ambitious program, into the details of which we need not enter here. Despite its

---

* A reprint of the seven-volume set, as originally published in 1925-1942, has been announced by the Genealogical Publishing Company of Baltimore.

pretentiousness, it seems fair, for several reasons, to include it in our account of commercial houses. It ultimately went out of business.

In the foregoing discussion of commercial firms, it has not been our intention to criticize those which conducted a legitimate business. It is only when they have made a false pretense of offering research facilities that they render themselves liable to criticism. Some years ago, such a case was brought to my notice. A woman had signed a contract with a commercial firm which offered at a stated price to trace her ancestry and publish a book devoted to it. A relative became suspicious and started research in original documentary sources. The book meanwhile was published, containing many notable lines (beautifully embellished with colored coats-of-arms) which her relative could prove were not in her ancestry at all; and a law-suit resulted.

In their legitimate field the commercial houses perform a very useful service. An example is the Genealogical Publishing Company of Baltimore which in recent years has reprinted by offset many genealogical reference books, including ship passenger lists, abstracts of wills, marriage licenses, court records, compendium genealogies, and so on, which have been long out of print, and thus made them available to such libraries and individuals as desire to obtain copies. Its affiliate firms, the Heraldic Book Company and the Regional Publishing Company, have reprinted reference books on heraldry and local and state history. This publishing company has in some instances obtained copies for reproduction which contain some corrections and additions as marginalia. In others they have incorporated material published later such as additions and corrections from genealogical periodicals and other sources. Where necessary and economical, they have also added indexes to books. They have also published offprints of records in genealogical and historical periodicals and in the printed state archives.

Generally speaking, the work done by commercial houses does not conflict with that done by professional genealogists. Clients of the former desire coats-of-arms or illustrious ancestry—at least the shadow of illustrious ancestry; or they are satisfied to accept what is found in print. Clients of the latter desire to ascertain the truth, lead where it may, and are willing to finance a scholarly investigation based on the original documentary evidence, in order to unearth genuine historic fact. Both classes of client pay for what they get; and they both get what they pay for.

It is a pity that so little research is done from first sources and information produced which is dependable. So many of the present acting genealogical bureaus are merely compendiums of already published material. They expend vast sums in the work, but they produce not a single new fact and do not even correct material submitted. It is enough to make a real honest-to-goodness genealogist throw a fit.

—*W. B. B. in The Boston Transcript.*

Sept. 17, 1930.

X

THE CLIENT

Come now, and let us reason together.
—Isaiah.

The clientele of a successful genealogist is scattered through-out the country, and it is only occasionally that he has the opportunity to meet a client personally. This necessitates the handling of negotiations by correspondence. After a genealogist has written giving his rates, explaining that he cannot furnish what is desired without research, and estimating the probable cost of the work, a considerable inroad has been made on his time. It is not merely that he has written one, two, or three letters. He has had to consider the correspondent's problem, consult his notes and perhaps his books, study the best approach to the problem, and estimate the expense if his advice is accepted and if — a large if — he gets the commission.

After the genealogist has done all this, the prospective client may decide that the suggested cost is more than he cares to spend, and drop the matter. This is his privilege, and he is the best judge of what he can afford. Nevertheless it means, in the aggregate, much wasted time for the genealogist. In addition, letters are often received of the "thank-you-and-cordially-yours" type. Some write to offer the genealogist data they have collected, and to request information in exchange. If the genealogist can furnish the desired information, and is foolish enough to accept such an offer, the other party gets precisely what he wants, while the genealogist receives material that is useless to him unless some later client happens to want just that material. And even then, he may not dare use it if it is unreferenced or carries the least taint of inaccuracy.

The proper answer to this kind of offer is to write that you are not interested in the material offered, but that you will consider an exchange if the writer can solve a problem of yours with record proof; and select one of your most difficult unsolved problems. Thus, politely, you will rid yourself of one of the worst pests known to the profession. This sort of person would not scruple to ask a minister to marry him without a fee, but offer in exchange to give him some notes that might someday come in handy for a sermon. Yet, after all, most such incidents no doubt are due to thoughtlessness and a lack of understanding of the genealogist's point of view.

I once received a sixteen-page letter, written by hand, which I ploughed through, seeking to digest the stated facts of the problem, until I reached the last page, on which the writer expressed her gratitude if I could <u>give</u> her the desired information. It was one of a dozen letters received in that mail, and I fear I was more curt than is my custom in replying. Now, when a letter is long, I look at the last page first.

My own mail, because of the fact that I published a magazine, was perhaps heavier than that of the average genealogist; there were many weeks when it required two full days, working with a typist, simply to take care of correspondence. Again, most genealogists have no office outside the home, and this subjects them to many interruptions. Like all professional people whose income depends entirely on personal services, if they are ill and unable to work they are earning nothing at just the time when they need increased earnings to offset increased expenses.

These factors are mentioned for the benefit of readers of the client class, who may unreflectingly suppose that because a genealogist asks so much an hour, he is high-priced and must earn a marvelous income. What a genealogist receives for an hour's work is not the sole consideration; his income is conditioned by the number of free hours per day or per week that are available for paying work.

When writing to a genealogist who is a stranger, the prospective client should ask his rates and write briefly, yet giving the essential names, dates and localities, to explain the object of the proposed search. It should always be specified whether the search is for the purpose of proving eligibility to a certain society. If satisfied with the genealogist's reply and terms, a second letter should give more complete details, particularly any information the genealogist may have requested; should specify what, if any, research has already been made, so that work need not be duplicated; and should fix a maximum limit of expense not to be exceeded. The genealogist should then report results when the problem is solved, or if not solved, when the limit set is reached.

No genealogist likes to report failure. Those who have their ancestry traced do not always understand the conditions under which research is made. There are many classes of original records which may have a bearing on the solution of a problem. These are apt to be located in different places, and the genealogist has to use his judgment which to examine first. Often, however, it is a matter of sheer luck whether the desired proofs are in the first class of records consulted, or in the last. Not infrequently, it is necessary to collect the evidence bit by bit, here and there, until a case has been built up and a conclusion proved. If the desired information is found in a family or town history, it is because in the past the compiler did this fundamental research work and kindly made the results public in a book.

The only question then is, whether this printed work is adequate and to be relied on, or whether it is the haphazard product of a novice. An experienced genealogist should be able to advise whether to accept the printed word or not; though it is always well to remember that no genealogical book is perfect, and all the genealogist can be expected to say of a book is that it is usually correct. If original records are searched without success, the genealogist should not be blamed unless his report indicates inadequacy on his part.

The genealogist, in dealing with a client, should not make his letters too curt. A friendly attitude, and a willingness to explain in some detail what he has done and why, should make for good feeling on both sides. If the searcher is by nature too cold and reserved, he should do his utmost to assume the virtue he lacks and put something of the personal touch into his letters. If he keeps making an effort to write a friendly letter, not familiar of course, but with a little human feeling in it, he may find that his mental attitude will change accordingly. Many genealogists lead a lonely sort of existence, completely bound up in their work. Those of whom this is true can offset it somewhat by making friends of their clients, even it be only by correspondence. And from the business angle, it will be found that clients often come back year after year to genealogists whose letters strike a responsive chord.

Remember (I am talking now to the young genealogist) that many of your clients live far from record sources or at any rate have never attempted original research personally, and in consequence have no conception of what you have to do to find what they want, or what difficulties are apt to be encountered. If you fail, do not write a line or two and expect the client to come back to you for more. Explain that the church records of this parish were burned; or that you had to stop over night in that town and thus add to the expense of the trip. Tell the truth; but tell it. If a good client, especially one whose searches have not been very successful of late, now wants information which it happens you already have in your notes, give him a "break" and let him have it at moderate cost. You will not gain in the end by being too grasping.

As stated in the chapter on "Genealogy as a Profession," conditions are unsatisfactory because so many have flocked into the profession who lack the aptitude and training for this type of work. A majority of the client class have no knowledge of proper methods of research, and if the genealogist gives them what they want, naturally they are satisfied. But sometimes clients are critical; and it would be well if they were more so. Over fifty years ago, a gentleman in Pennsylvania employed a New York genealogist who was well known and even had quite a reputation at that time, to trace a certain line, and she sent him a pedigree covering six generations. He noticed that in one generation, the son was born a few years before the marriage of the alleged parents. His suspicions were aroused, and he sent the pedigree to another genealogist, who discovered that in three generations out of the six, the supposed son was not the child of the parents assigned to him.

It is small wonder if many jump to the conclusion, after such an experience, that nothing is certain, and that what one genealogist affirms another will deny. A public official in a town where I once searched records said to me, "Well, genealogy is mostly guess-work, isn't it?" I answered, "Yes, if the genealogist prefers guessing."

As a matter of fact, a large percentage of lines can be traced back to the first settlers, some easily, others with difficulty. It is the difficult lines which most often the skilled genealogist is called upon to solve, and this of itself explains why his efforts are not invariably successful. Many lines can be proved by legal evidence as surely as titles to real estate can be proved. Land titles are traced through land and probate records; occasionally, there is a flaw in the title, usually because someone failed to have an instrument recorded. Similarly, a genealogical line cannot always be established by legal proof because of deficiencies in the records. But a skilled searcher resents having his work characterized as "guess-work." If properly done, it is just as certain as the work of the title searcher, and requires fully as much care and knowledge. The difference is that the title searcher is a trained lawyer; too often, the genealogist is an untrained enthusiast.

Nevertheless, standards have grown higher, and the capable genealogists of today are the equal of the capable genealogist of the past, and furthermore have increased facilities with which to work. The New York genealogist referred to above would hardly achieve much of a reputation today. Although competition in other lines of work, and the allurement of the genealogical profession, attract into it some incompetents, they will either grow in competence as they gain experience, or will leave the profession and drift into other lines of work. There is still room in the profession for young genealogists of real ability and aptitude.

How can the prospective client pick a suitable genealogist? If possible, choose one who lives near the ancestral town or at least within the ancestral state. It is obvious that this should save travel costs, since any capable genealogist will wish to consult the contemporary record sources. Some genealogists, in fact, specialize in the records of their own region. Naturally, you will not employ a northern genealogist to undertake research in the South, or a southern genealogist to work in the North. In addition to the expense involved in reaching the records, there are often differences, which have to be learned, in the method of keeping records in different sections of the country.

In 1965 a Board for Certification of Genealogists was set up, with headquarters at 1307 New Hampshire Avenue, N. W., Washington, D. C. 20036. The qualification of applicants is determined by an inspection of their printed works or by an examination. Successful applicants are authorized to use the initials C. G. (Certified Genealogist), those who are capable of giving full genealogical service, or G. R. S. (Genealogical Record Searcher), those who search original sources such as census, pension, probate, land, and other records, but do not attempt to organize the material into pedigrees or family histories. The use of these initials ought to give a client some measure of protection against incompetents, although no guarantee of proficiency is given. Many genealogists in active practice have submitted their credentials and are entitled to use these initials. Quite likely a few who have built up a high reputation over the years have not bothered to apply to the Board. It is suggested that clients select either a genealogist who has been approved by the Board or one whose work has long been favorably known. But in neither case can work be assured that will satisfy the client.

There is one subject on which many people who are genealogically inclined feel strongly and seek professional advice, but which really does not concern the genealogist. This is the question of the correct spelling of the family name. I have been criticized for presuming to spell Granniss with but one 's' and Tallmadge with but one 'l'. A Mr.

Clarke wishes to have it understood that his name is not Clark. The answer to queries and criticisms of this type is: the correct way to spell your surname is the way you yourself spell it. We are reminded of old Wait Munson who insisted on his name being spelled "Weait" because "he liked the vowels in."

Every man is privileged to spell his own name as he sees fit. But because you and perhaps your father and grandfather spelled the name a certain way, is no reason for being concerned to prove that your first American ancestor spelled it the same way. It is a matter of small importance whether he did or not, and our first American ancestors were too much occupied with serious matters to worry much about how their names were spelled. The spelling in vital records is not conclusive, since it may have been the error of a clerk. The spelling on gravestones is not always conclusive, for stone-cutters made many mistakes. Even an autograph is not conclusive unless the writer was a man of some education, for oftentimes men spelled their names differently in different signatures. Finally, if you prove to your satisfaction how your first American ancestor spelled his name, it does not follow that his English forbears spelled it the same way. The father of the first American Alling spelled his name Allen in signing his will.

To show what a role the lack of education plays in such matters, there was a soldier in the Revolutionary War who bestowed the name of Marquis Lafayette on a son. The family moved to the frontier, where little schooling was to be had; and the son who had received the distinguished name, wishing to pass it along to his own son, had him christened Marcus Fayette. The name Marcus was handed down in the family, apparently in ignorance of its origin.

The amateur or professional who gives undue importance to variations of spelling reveals himself as a novice. However, care must be exercised not to confuse similar names which were really distinct; and in copying from record sources, the exact spellings found in the record should be followed.

A large number of Americans seem to be bewitched by heraldic devices, and to meet the demand, many genealogists dabble in heraldry and tell their clients what coats-of-arms they are entitled to. Since heraldry is not an American institution, there is nothing to prevent a person from appropriating any insignia of this kind that take the fancy. But establishing a right by European usage to a particular coat-of-arms is quite another story. Identity of <u>surname</u> is not sufficient; identity of <u>family</u> is required. It is therefore necessary to trace the American family, generation by generation, back to a European progenitor who had a valid claim to the arms.

The great majority of early American families were not armigerous; even if they were, unless the ancestry has been traced in England and can be found in print with valid evidence fully presented, it is necessary to have special research made on the other side of the ocean. Some American families used heraldic devices in the first or second generation in this country, and it is generally conceded that this gives their descendants a good claim to the use of the same devices. But as a rule, conscientious genealogists should tell their clients frankly that they are not in a position to pass on a claim to the use of a coat-of-arms, and that unless the clients are satisfied to adopt a device of their own fabrication, the only recourse is research abroad which forty-nine times out of fifty will not result in establishing the right to a foreign coat-of-arms.

> *Kind hearts are more than coronets,*
> *And simple faith, than Norman blood.*
> *—Tennyson.*

XI
SOURCE MATERIAL — PRINTED

The nearest way to come at glory, is to do that for conscience which we do for glory.—Benjamin Franklin.

Genealogists may be divided roughly into two classes: library workers and archivists. When interest is first aroused in the subject of genealogy, one naturally seeks out a large library and searches for published matter concerning the families in which one is interested. The reason for this is obvious. Most people are not fortunate enough to reside in the region where many of their forefathers lived, and in consequence the original archives are not immediately accessible. In addition, it requires, or should require, long training before one is competent to handle original sources intelligently. For this is genuine research, unearthing clues, facts, and records from diverse sources, and fitting them together into a coherent whole; and it demands much special knowledge, and a certain type of ability.

A majority of those who hunt ancestors never graduate from the library stage of research, and unfortunately this has been true of some who set themselves up as professionals. Mr. William Bradford Browne, a genealogist of repute, wrote as follows in the Pilgrim News Letter: "When I enter a genealogical room and see the many workers industriously copying from the printed records, I have a feeling almost of dismay, realizing that each one is perhaps adding to the already hopeless tangle of twisted pedigrees."

While there have always been a few capable genealogists at any given period during the past hundred years or so, the more recent years have seen the rise of a modern school of genealogists who demand a higher standard of accuracy than has been customary, and who insist on the application of scientific and scholarly methods of research. Despite much improvement, the old haphazard methods are still prevalent, largely because the genealogical public is still to some extent uninformed as to proper methods of research.

Printed material nevertheless has its uses, and should not be neglected, even by those professionals who are able to consult the original archives. As briefly as possible, I will describe the different types of published sources.

There are several periodicals which contain useful data. The oldest is The New England Historical and Genealogical Register, which for many years past has been under able editorship. The standard of accuracy is high, because the editors have not knowingly accepted articles from any but proficient writers. This is not to say that every statement made in the Register is invariably correct, because in well over a century, articles by thousands of writers have been published, and not all of them were equally proficient. Furthermore, both methods and facilities of research have improved of late years. Nevertheless, a very large amount of valuable and in the main accurate information may be found in this publication, and that in the first fifty volumes is made readily accessible by a voluminous general index. The separate indices of the later volumes have to be consulted, so far as individual names are concerned, but an abridged Index to Volumes 51 through 112 published by Margaret Wellington Parsons in 1959 is most valuable as a guide to genealogies, biographies, records of places and topics.

The New York Genealogical and Biographical Record ranks very high among periodicals, and occupies the primary place as far as New York State is concerned. It has not restricted itself too closely to its chosen field, and it is rather surprising to find how much concerning New England families has appeared in its pages. Of recent years, its copies and abstracts of original records have been so useful that the library worker should not fail to consult the separate indices of each volume.

The Genealogical Magazine of New Jersey since 1925 has published many records of that state. John Frederick Dorman's The Virginia Genealogist has done the same for Virginia since 1957. The Genealogical Society of Pennsylvania for years has published a fine magazine devoted to that state. The National Genealogical Society Quarterly, founded in 1912, for a number of years has been under able editorship and published articles of value. The magazine of the Detroit Society for Genealogical Research merits special mention. In 1932 the present writer founded The American Genealogist for the express purpose of seeking to improve genealogical standards. In this he was greatly aided by a few genealogists of established reputation, and quite a few well-known genealogists of today had their first articles published in this organ. Since the end of 1965 it has been continued under a new editor (Dr. George E. McCracken) but with similar policies.

In recent years there has been a spate of quarterlies and bulletins issued by historical and genealogical societies in all parts of the country; Texas has nearly a dozen and California several. It is next to impossible for the amateur seeking to trace his own ancestry to consult them all. But he should not neglect to consult the periodicals which are general in scope and which have a high reputation, nor those which relate to the localities in which his forebears lived.

The Boston Evening Transcript for many years published, twice weekly, a genealogical department containing queries, answers and notes. Some of the contributors were skilled genealogists, others inexperienced gropers after knowledge. Valuable clues, and occasionally much dependable data, can be gleaned from these pages, if one learns to recognize the contributions of those who searched original sources and based their statements on substantial rock. A complete run, 1904-1941, is available on microcards from the Godfrey Memorial Library, Middletown, Conn. Other newspapers have or have had genealogical columns, but none with the national prestige which the Transcript enjoyed in its heyday.

It is easy to overlook valuable records published in various periodicals, because of deficient indexing or the lack of general indices.

The periodical indexes published by the present writer and his successors help to supply this deficiency, but they are not full name indexes. For some books, a full name index is supplied by Fremont Rider's American Genealogical Biographical Index, also obtainable from the Godfrey Memorial Library.

Several States have published their Colonial records, and these are standard authorities and the proper source for civil services and military appointments. Many town and church records have been published. Here we have original records, correct except for possible misreadings and typographical errors. Such errors are more common in this type of publication than is generally realized. The most experienced experts cannot always read a name correctly unless they are guided by a knowledge of the families whose records they are copying. The name John, for example, can be read Jolin if in the original record there happened to be an ink dot over the lower part of the 'h'. There is a book of printed vital records where this mistake actually occurs several times.

Some books of town records contain verbatim copies, which are indexed; and this is the best method. Others, to make it easier for the student to find desired entries, arrange the vital statistics alphabetically. On the face of it, this might be supposed to be the most useful system; but it does not work out so in practice. The births are arranged alphabetically by the names of the children; if you want the children of given parents, it is necessary to hunt through all the births of that surname and pick them out individually. Oftentimes, in the original record, an entire family group was entered at one time on the same page. When the children are split up and arranged alphabetically, there is not the same assurance that they were children of the same parents.

This applies even more forcibly to church records. When several children of the same parents were presented for baptism on the same date, the recording minister customarily entered the names in order of birth, from the eldest to the youngest. When in printing they are split up and arranged alphabetically, there is nothing to guide the searcher as to their relative ages, which it is often important to know.

The first federal census (1790) of heads of families is one of the most useful source materials to be found in print, as it definitely locates each male head of a household in a definite town, and shows the general distribution of surnames. The work of preparing these records for publication was very carefully done, yet many errors in reading names appear. It is of course impossible to read thousands of names which were written in many handwritings by census takers of 1790, not all of whom were notable for education or even literacy, without error. The wonder is that these printed census records are so generally reliable. *

Town histories and county histories often contain genealogical sections. Despite shining exceptions, publications of this class do

---

* The twelve volumes of the 1790 federal census, as originally published in 1907-1908, have been reprinted by the Genealogical Publishing Company of Baltimore.

not rank high for either accuracy or completeness. Many contain the records only of selected families. The task of compiling, that is, of arranging the vital statistics which the author has copied, often suffers from being based almost exclusively on the vital records, without the aid of probate and land records. Some books of this sort are very accurate as to names and dates, but utterly untrustworthy as to lines of descent; for it is almost impossible to arrange the correct sequence from father to sons and grandchildren without the wills and distributions in the probate records, which show what family groups belonged together.

Most of the mistakes which are found so frequently in town histories are of the following order. John Jones, let us say, had births of children recorded, the eldest being a namesake who was born in 1710. In 1731 there is record of marriage of John Jones, and another marriage is recorded as occurring in 1735. Overlapping children of one or more men named John Jones are recorded in the 1730's and 1740's. John, Sr., perhaps had a second wife and some of the children belonged to him. Or did John, Jr., marry twice, and can all the children be assigned to him? Very often, which solution is adopted is a mere matter of guessing, unless the wills of the two Johns are consulted and the children belonging to each ascertained beyond question. If no will is found, then perhaps the children of one of the Johns made a mutual agreement for the distribution of his lands, and this we may find in the land records.

When the historian of a town is writing up the records of all of the families of his town, it requires years of labor to cover the probate and land records as well as the vital statistics, and even if able and willing to devote the time to it, the writer may lack the knowledge and training to make the best use of the records he does cover. But most town historians have not even made the effort, and books of this type should never be relied on too far unless they bear evidence of having been based on a thorough search of all record sources.

It might be supposed that the historian of a single family would fine it possible to search original records thoroughly; but that is not the fact. A large majority of family histories are compiled by some member of the family who, notwithstanding the interest and enthusiasm he brings to the task, and the natural ability he may possess, lacks experience in this type of research. He may in addition lack the type of mentality which it requires. If he happens to live far from the old towns where the early generations of the family resided, the difficulties of his undertaking are increased, and often he is utterly without realization of the many avenues open to research.

The issuing of a family history is a major expense. Printing costs are high, and the sales of the volume are necessarily limited. In an undertaking which involves in total many hundreds, and often several thousands of dollars, it seems a pity to save a small part of the total cost by neglecting to obtain readily accessible records which would add far more to the intrinsic value of the book than a handsome appearance, desirable though the latter be.

Yet volume after volume is turned out at large cost of publication, in blissful ignorance of record sources, only scratching the surface of the research, full of erroneous deductions and inconsistencies, bearing evidence of rank amatourishness. To be sure, it would be quite expensive to cover all record sources thoroughly, and it may be taken for granted that the compiler must keep the expenso within certain limits. But many compilers never even make a beginning, and apparently never even learn that record sources are available. Too often, they are satisfied to follow what is found in print on the early generations, in total ignorance of its trustworthiness, and to reconcile all difficulties they encounter by assumptions and guesses. In view of this situation, it is remarkable that so many good family histories have been written, and that the average one is even as good as it is.

Can the amateur write a good family history? Decidedly, yes. The only difference between the amateur and the professional is, that the former does not work for a fee. If an amateur possesses the ability and training, and if he lives near enough to original sources to learn to use them with facility, he may become more proficient than some professionals who lack these advantages. Ono of the best family histories I have used was written by an amateur; he was trained as a lawyer, had written several genealogies, and used original sources to the fullest extent. Another amateur, a prominent attorney with whom genealogy is a hobby, has compiled the families of one of the old towns. To this end, he copied vital and church records, visited cemeteries, and worked systematically through the land and probate records. With his legal training, when he states he has proved a certain point, I know that he means proved.

The genealogical student must be very cautious in his use of family histories, remembering the conditions under which most of them were produced. This caution applies chiefly to the earlier, let us say the first six, generations. Even the poorest genealogy contains data of value, for the compiler obtained information from family sources that is not available to us in any other way. In deciding how far back on a certain line it is advisable to trust a certain genealogy, particularly when the earlier sections do not look trustworthy, the date when the book was published must always be considered. If published fifty or sixty years ago, information was often obtained from aged descendants then living, and of course their memory went further back than would that of elderly descendants today.

The great compilation of Savage (Genealogical Dictionary of New England) and other works of this class deserve more than the passing mention we are able to give them. Savage was a pioneer, working without the facilities which are open to genealogists today; and he displayed marvelous critical acumen and judgment in handling the material that was then accessible. Nevertheless, after more than a century Savage's work is antiquated and must be amplified by that of many searchers who have combed smaller fields with greater thoroughness. His Dictionary remains, however, a standard work, and will always be serviceable to genealogical students who know within what limits it is advisable to use it. *

In addition to the old-style family genealogies which aim to trace all the descendants in the male line of an original settler to the present day, another type of genealogy has become popular. This is the pedigree book which traces all the American ancestors of a present-day descendant. No one family can be accorded very full treatment, but often valuable data are presented pertaining to the branch in which the compiler is interested, covering from one to several generations. Some books of this type are poorly compiled, and based almost entirely on inferior printed sources. It is difficult to see what advantage there is in merely reprinting what is already available in print, even though the immediate family of the compiler appears more fully than elsewhere.

Many fine examples could be given of this type of compilation, where the research was made in original sources. The two volumes of "Goodwin and Morgan Ancestral Lines" compiled by Mr. Frank Farnsworth Starr set a high mark for meticulous accuracy which perhaps has been equalled but could scarcely be surpassed. The brochures published more recently by Mr. Walter Goodwin Davis are of this type, and excellent models for those who are planning similar compilations; as is also the "Dawes-Gates Ancestral Lines," compiled by Mrs. Mary Walton Ferris of Chicago.

For an example of a family history, accurate and complete, well arranged and indexed, the reader is referred to "The Trowbridge Genealogy," published in 1908 by Mr. Francis Bacon Trowbridge. For this book, the most thorough research in original sources was made, and the finished product presented in condensed form without much quotation of wills and deeds. Many compilers of such works prefer to print copies of the wills of the members of the earlier generations. When the descendants are at all completely traced, the resulting volume becomes so immense that it is difficult to afford the space for wills and other documents. When they are not included, the user of the book can accept the conclusions given by the compiler if he is a veteran worker in the field of genealogy; but if he is not, abstracts of the original documents add to the reader's confidence.

How can the searcher distinguish between the carefully compiled book which is generally to be trusted, and the book issued by a novice or uncritical genealogist which is likely to contain many errors? Much experience in using books of all grades of perfection or imperfection is required to give the mind of the student a fine critical edge. The genealogist who has worked much in original sources and who has compared what the records contain with what is found in print is better qualified to sift the chaff from the wheat than one who has utilized only printed sources. As a standard for comparison, familiarize yourself with family histories issued by the most reputable compilers, such as those of the late J. Gardner Bartlett; study the arrangement, complete-

---

* This four-volume set, as originally published in 1860-1862, with the addition of "Genealogical Notes and Errata" and a "Genealogical Cross Index of the Four Volumes," has been reprinted by the Genealogical Publishing Company of Baltimore.

ness, and type of authorities quoted.

Always distrust statements that are vague, without dates, or undocumented. Check whatever dates are available, and see whether the line of descent given is humanly possible. Consider what type of book you are examining. If it is a family history, look through the first five generations and find out whether nearly all the males are accounted for and their branches carried on. If not, the chances are that the research of the compiler was far from thorough.

A few concrete examples will help the novice more than a discussion of general considerations. Since the aim is to aid the novice, and not to criticise the work of others, the names of authors or compilers will not be mentioned, merely the titles of the books from which the examples have been drawn.

"History of Wallingford, Conn." (1870), page 852, states: Maj. Thomas Miles of New Haven, married Abigail Mix, daughter of Thomas Mix, Sept. 7, 1709. His father, Richard Miles, died in New Haven in 1663, and his mother, Mrs. Katherine Miles, died in Wallingford, Jan. 27, 1683, ae. 95 yrs.

It is hoped that the novice will criticise these statements for himself before reading on. Without any special research, it can be concluded that Thomas Miles was not son of Richard and Katherine. The latter, if her age is correctly stated, was born 1588, and her alleged son married 121 years later. Thomas did not marry until 46 years after the death of his alleged father. It should not take the student long to reach the conclusion that generations have been omitted, if indeed Thomas belonged to this family at all.

"Winthrop-Babcock Genealogy" (1927), page 506, assigns an ancestral line to Captain John Underhill, a prominent early settler, which we summarize thus: Timotheus Underhill of Yorkshire, father of John (born 1284), father of Nathaniel (born 1324, resided at Wolcesboughton, County Stratford), father of William (of Wolverhampton 1423), father of Edward (died in Holland), who by wife Mary Moseley (died in Coventry) was father of Captain John (born at Bagington, Warwickshire, England, 5 Oct. 1597).

Nearly everything that could be wrong with an English ancestral line is to be seen in this Underhill pedigree. John's birth date is stated, but as births were not recorded in England, it should have been a baptismal date if from a parish register. No dates are given for the parents, not even that of their marriage, and no wills are cited. The pedigree strays all over the map of England, fails to specify in what county Wolverhampton was located, and invents a non-existent county (Stratford). Finally, John's birth is stated as 273 years later than that of his alleged great-grandfather, which necessitates an average age of 91 years at the birth of the son for the fathers in three successive generations. It should be apparent at a glance that the pedigree is worthless.

"History of Ancient Woodbury, Connecticut" (1854), Volume 1, page 663, sets forth a line of descent from George Preston, of Valley Field, who was created a baronet of Nova Scotia in 1637, through his second son William (died 1685), to the latter's third son John, whose son William emigrated to America in 1635.

Here too, a glance shows the inherent improbability of the ancestral line assigned to the American settler. A little investigation reveals that there really was a Preston family of Valley Field, and that George was created a baronet in 1637; but it also shows that the age of William, the emigrant, was given as 44 years in the 1635 shipping list which is to be found in print. Hence, William was born about 1591, some 46 years before his alleged great-grandfather was created a baronet. This is an example of a practice that has been all too common in the past. Somebody consulted a work on the peerage, found a William Preston in the titled family, and without a particle of evidence, without even a study of the dates to check possibilities, appropriated this William as the founder of the American family.

"Genealogical and Family History of the State of Connecticut" (1911), volume 1, page 500, contains a Bassett line, beginning with John of New Haven, and continuing through Robert of New Haven and Stratford, and the latter's alleged son, Captain Samuel of Derby.

Rather full information of each generation is given, and a novice might not readily detect misstatements. The book, however, was issued by a commercial house, and therefore, despite much data of undoubted value, its statements need to be carefully checked before acceptance. The novice here should consult other printed sources, and will find that their statements do not agree with those given above. It is then a question of following the best printed accounts, or of going to the original records for independent verification.

To show what sort of errors are often encountered in works of this class, the following misstatements in the account of the Bassett family will be pointed out. It was not Robert of the second generation who lived at Stratford; he lived at Stamford. It was his son, a second Robert, who lived at Stratford, and it was this omitted Robert who was father of Captain Samuel. The children of the first Robert were thus stated: "Robert; Sarah, married Jacob Walker; daughter, married Henry Tiff, November 8, 1673; Samuel." There was no son Samuel; as already mentioned, he was actually a son of the second Robert. There was no daughter who married Jacob Walker. It was Sarah who married on 8 Jan. 1673/4, Henry Hitt. Both the date and the husband's name had been misread. Of Captain Samuel the book states: "He married Deborah Newton, from near Newtown, January 1, 1719." Orcutt's history of Derby, published years before, correctly gave the line of Captain Samuel through the two Roberts, and also correctly gave the marriage of Captain Samuel to Deborah Bennett, not Newton.

Of course, mistakes are found, but less frequently, even in books based largely on original records; and this is apt to be true of books compiled by those who have had too little experience to interpret the records and extract their true meaning. One gentleman who issued a little book on the Beecher family boasted that he had not accepted the many erroneous statements to be found in print, but had gone to the records for everything. Unfortunately, he did not know that the term "cousin" in the old records most often signified a nephew or niece. In consequence, he misinterpreted the will of a childless Beecher who left legacies to several "cousins." To account for them, the compiler invented a nameless uncle who had died and left those children mentioned in the will. Yet the compiler already had the same names placed correctly as nephews and nieces of the testator.

"The Bulkeley Family" (1875), compiled by the author of several other family histories, contains a mistake that may have been due to a similar cause. There were in Fairfield, Conn., two Peter Bulkeleys, cousins whose ages were only five months apart. As was customary, the elder was called "Senior," and the younger, "Junior" or "Second," to distinguish them in the records. These terms did not then imply a certain kind of relationship, as that of father and son, or even any relationship at all. One of the Peters was son of an earlier Peter, and the writer of the family history assumed that he must have been the one called "Junior." Actually, he was the one called "Senior," as a careful study of the land records proves.

In general, view printed sources as clue books, not as dispensers of the eternal verities.

> *It must be true. I seen it in print.*
> *—Favorite Proverb of Morons.*

XII

SOURCE MATERIAL — ORIGINAL

Take ye the sum of all the congregation of the children of Israel, after their families, by the house of their fathers.—Numbers.

And Abraham begat Isaac.
—Chronicles.

When it comes to searching original records, the most important factor is the ability of the genealogist who does the searching. Again we should like to quote Mr. William Bradford Browne, who states that genealogy is a science "which requires years of preparation, and is only successfully acquired by a person naturally adapted to its study, and to whom its drudgery is pleasure and not work. It means the power to read or decipher ancient records, to understand their meaning, to read them with the understanding of obsolete meanings. It means a knowledge of law, sufficient to understand the why and wherefore of papers of a legal nature..... It requires the intimate knowledge of towns, counties and states, so that the genealogist knows where certain records are at stated periods, and how these towns and counties have been divided and at what times ..... It requires the knowledge of the changes of the calendar from the old arrangement to the new."

No genealogist is so proficient that he can search records in all localities equally well. Many now specialize in certain areas with the records of which they are thoroughly familiar, and often they can obtain better results and at less cost in their special territory than could any other genealogist less familiar with it. For many years I employed other genealogists in other sections of the country as occasion arose, and was employed at times by other genealogists who desired research in my special field. This saves traveling expenses at least, and usually the arrangement has worked out well. But there are not always competent searchers in all sections, or one does not always learn of them. Again, a professional genealogist, dependent on his work for a livelihood, may not feel he can afford to turn a piece of research over to a genealogist living in the proper territory unless at the moment he has enough commissions that he can work on personally.

There are several genealogical handbooks which give information as to where records are located in certain sections. None that I have seen gives the reader much idea as to just how he should work with original records when he has located them. This is a matter in which experience is the best teacher; but to give the general reader an idea as to how problems are solved, a few "case histories" will be set forth in the next chapter, following each step of the research.

Here we cannot even attempt to instruct the reader as to the location of different classes of records throughout the entire country.

Frankly, I admit that I am not competent to cover so wide a field, and it would be difficult to find a genealogist who could do so. My object here is merely to give the inexperienced amateur and the general reader an idea of what sort of archives exist from which genealogical information can be extracted. For this purpose, I shall limit myself to the archives to be found in Connecticut, the territory with which I am most familiar.

Many searchers feel, when they visit an historical society and examine its manuscript collections, that they are utilizing original sources. This is rarely the truth, although a few original documents, sometimes the original of a church record, are on deposit in the libraries of historical societies. But the collections consist mainly of copies made by various persons, some by good copyists and others by copyists not so good, of certain original records.

The Connecticut Historical Society in Hartford has a most valuable collection, especially copies of church records from all over the State; there are also many compilations, arranged by various genealogists, both professional and amateur, who worked in the original sources. It is often useful to consult these collections, provided that one bears it in mind that these are not original records and may now and again contain errors or misleading information. Whenever one uses the manuscript collections of professional genealogists which have been acquired by historical societies it should never be forgotten that these were the genealogist's working notes, drawn from many sources, both original and printed, and that the genealogist himself would probably not have given out the information as it stands to clients; he knew how to use his own notes, and did not expect that they would be used by strangers, or they might not have been left in their present shape. While useful as clues, they should not therefore be accepted as invariably correct.

Other historical societies throughout the State also have valuable manuscript collections, with which the searcher must familiarize himself if he expects to make much use of them. A professional genealogist should never give a client material that comes from such collections without specifying that it was taken from a copy and may be subject to correction.

The most extensive collections of archives is to be found in the State Library at Hartford. Several State Librarians, notably Headly, Godard and Brewster, labored ceaselessly for years until the Connecticut State Library has become second to none in the country for the extent and value of its archives. We are now dealing at last with original records, and must attempt in limited space to convey some idea of the wealth of material available in the Library.

Large numbers of documents are filed in big "scrap books," classified by subject, as for example ecclesiastical affairs, military affairs, private controversies, Revolutionary War, crimes and misdemeanors, etc., and are copiously indexed.

A large majority of the probate districts have deposited their files at the State Library, where they can readily be consulted by use of the card index covering the whole collection. There are also separate index volumes for each district. At the time of writing there are still districts which have not deposited their files, and many have deposited only up to 1850. Those not at the library have to be consulted wherever those Probate Courts are located. Many of the districts cover more territory than a single town, and several towns at various times have been shifted from one probate district to another. The searcher who hopes to achieve the best results must study the history of the probate districts, in order to learn where to look for the estates in which he is interested. The Church of Latter-day Saints has provided the Library with microfilms of both probate and land record volumes up to 1850, arranged by probate districts and by towns.

The probate record volumes often contain matter that is not in the files. This is because in the past documents have been stolen from the files in some districts where laxity formerly prevailed; some were accidentally destroyed; and in addition, certain entries were made in the record volumes which never had corresponding documents in the files. The files also contain papers of which no copy was ever made in the record volumes, such as unproved wills and other papers which were ordered filed without recording. Hence, one can never feel certain that he has all the information available unless both the files and the record volumes have been searched.

The early records of a number of churches, census records for several decades, photostatic copies of census records of other years, files of the Superior Court in which divorce petitions and other documents of interest to the genealogist may be found. Of special importance are the files and record volumes of the County Courts, which contain the early probate entries and much else of genealogical interest.

The generosity of Gen. Lucius B. Barbour has provided the Library with copies of the vital records to 1850 of every town in the State. In addition to verbatim copies, the entries have been alphabetically arranged in volumes for each separate town, and finally there is a card index, alphabetically arranged, covering the entire State. These copies and indices have not been verified, and errors of name and date occur. This does not affect the marvelous utility of the collection, and it saves the searcher much labor, time and expense. In specific searches, however, the professional genealogist working for clients should be watchful for possible error, remembering that here he is not dealing with original documents but with unverified copies.

The riches of the State Library have scarcely been sampled, but we must pass on to other places where original source material is to be found. The probate offices have already been mentioned. Wills and distributions are the sine qua non of family histories, and the compiler who attempts to write one without covering the probate records for the generations before 1850 would better write a novel instead, for his genealogy will contain much fiction.

Next to probate records, the land records are of most value to the genealogist. At least until the late 1700's, the conveyances of real estate teem with genealogical data. A man and his wife who conveyed together often specified that the land was set to her from the estate of her father and mention his name, thus solving the identity of a missing wife where no marriage record is found. Sometimes several heirs conveyed property together and stated their relationship to the former owner. Even the names of witnesses to deeds often provide clues, unless the justice or clerk who drew the document witnessed it; many witnesses were relatives or members of the household of the man who gave the deed. In Connecticut the land records are kept in each separate town; in many States they are kept at the county seat.

Vital records are also kept in each town, and if the genealogist is working in a stated town to cover the land and probate records, he may as well cover the original vital records there instead of using the copy at the State Library. He will thus make sure that nothing has been overlooked. The Library copy of the vital records may give Merritt for Merrill, Ady for Acly (Ackley), these being examples of mistakes I have personally noted.

There are fewer death records than entries of birth and marriage, and to make good the deficiency of the public records, the searcher should try to locate gravestones with the desired death records. Graveyards may not appeal to everyone as pleasant places for research, but stooping to read stones is excellent exercise for the genealogist who is growing stout at his desk. Many small graveyards are hard to find, and once an amateur friend gleefully drove me out not twenty miles from where I have worked all my life and showed me a graveyard I had never heard of. Copies of the stones in many cemeteries are to be seen in the various historical society libraries, and these should be consulted. Stones have fallen or the inscriptions have become illegible since earlier copies were made. The inscriptions in some graveyards have been printed in books or magazine articles. Stones standing in the 1930's were copied as a WPA project, and are indexed at the State Library.

Nothing is easier to misread than inscriptions and it requires long practice to become expert. The figure '4' in dates is oftentimes read as a '1' because the cross-bar was cut so lightly in comparison with the down-stroke that it has become almost obliterated. The wider spacing which the '4' required is in some cases the only clue to the correct figure.

The early County Court records contain many probate entries, because this Court sat part of the time as a Probate Court. The court orders, granting of administration, acceptance of the will and inventory, appointments of guardians, and orders of distribution (sometimes naming the heirs), were therefore entered in these volumes, while the wills, inventories, etc., were recorded in separate volumes which later passed into possession of the probate courts. Novices who are searching probate records rarely learn of this and by neglecting to consult the County Court records, fail to discover the most valuable information in intestate estates. The searcher should ascertain whether the County Court volumes are kept at the county seat or have been deposited at the State Library.

The church records supply many of the deficiencies of the public records, and the dates of baptism often have to be learned to approximate unrecorded dates of birth. Seven volumes of marriages from

Connecticut church records were published by Rev. Frederic W. Bailey, and are useful for quick reference despite a rather high percentage of error in reading names.* Since most church records are in the hands of the ecclesiastical societies, it is more difficult to gain access to them. Some are kept at the home of the minister or of the clerk of the church; others have been deposited for safe keeping in vaults. Copies of many church records can be seen at the historical societies; and the State Library has accepted for deposit the early original records of many Connecticut churches. Many have been indexed at the State Library.

While we have mentioned the most important original sources, others exist from which information can sometimes be gleaned. Files of old newspapers may be consulted for death notices or obituaries. Census and pension records at the National Archives in Washington should furnish their quota of information to the family historian. Shipping records of ports are another original source, not much utilized.

In working with the original sources, always make note of the volume and page of the record volume you take information from, or the name of the district and number of the file if you are using the probate files at the State Library. Personally I think such references are not of much importance. Lest I be burned in oil for this heresy, I will attempt to justify it. The only use for such a reference is if your client or the reader of your book should wish to verify your statement for himself. Since most of the record sources used are well indexed, he should have no difficulty in finding the record you quote, whether or not he has the exact reference. Naturally, if you find something by a page-by-page inspection of underlined early land records, you will want the reference so as to be able to find it again yourself or to enable your client to find it. Yet there is a risk involved. Very often, when an old volume is provided with a modern index, it is found that the original paging was inaccurate, page numbers being omitted or repeated, so the volume is repaged as a preliminary to indexing. When this happens, it makes a liar of any genealogist who has put in print a reference to the original page number. In one probate district I discovered that the volumes themselves had been renumbered; for an excellent abstract had been made of these records some thirty years before and the numbers of the volumes were then different from their present numbering.

Many books, full of poorly digested and arranged genealogical matter, are choked up with references to both original and printed sources. References do not in themselves guarantee the accuracy of the matter published. I would rather take the unreferenced word of a capable genealogist, either amateur or professional, that he had worked out a line and verified it from original records, than to trust an incompetent genealogist with all the references in the world.

---

* Early Connecticut Marriages as Found on Ancient Church Records Prior to 1800, with Additions, Corrections, and Introduction by Donald Lines Jacobus, originally published in 1896-1906, now reprinted in one volume by Genealogical Publishing Company of Baltimore.

Nevertheless, always take references when you work. It is customary; your client may expect it, and has the right to demand it.

While on the subject of heresies, I may as well close the chapter by getting another off my conscience. I don't think it makes an iota of difference whether a man who was born in 1700 or 1800 was born on the 17th day of July or on the 18th. Accuracy is important, yes; and the full date should always be copied just as it appears in the original record. But if you find a town record of death, and a church record of the same, and also a record of death from the man's stone, there is a very fair chance that you will have three different dates, all from original sources, any one of which may be correct. When I speak of inaccuracies in printed sources, I do not want to be understood as referring to slight discrepancies of this sort, where original records may quite possibly be at variance. These slight differences are of small import.

Some people swear by old Bible records. My experience with them — and I have had plenty of experience — is that as far as dates are concerned they are much less reliable than town or church records. Very often the entries were made after the entire family of children had been born, and in making the record the parents would figure that Tom was three years old in December and was two years younger than Nancy who was born in July, and so on from the youngest to the eldest. By the time the date was figured out for the eldest, it was sometimes a year or two out of the way. Comparison with church records of baptisms for the same family proves how often such mistakes occurred. In rectifying such source errors, always give the date as it appears in the original together with your correction.

The State Library, incidentally, has copies of many family and Bible records, and these private records have been typed and indexed. In many cases they fill in gaps in the public records, for after the Revolutionary War the recording of vital statistics fell off badly in most of New England. A law in 1820 in Connecticut required the recording of marriages, but the entry of births and deaths was not resumed until the 1840's.

For special conditions in other states and localities, a great deal of information will be found in Genealogical Research: Methods and Sources published by the American Society of Genealogists in 1960. Several good books on the subject have appeared in recent years. I confess a liking for the well-written Searching for Your Ancestors by Gilbert H. Doane (third edition, 1960). Exceptionally useful features are found in Archibald F. Bennett's A Guide for Genealogical Research (1951), E. Kay Kirkham's Research in American Genealogy (1956), and Noel C. Stevenson's Search and Research (second edition, 1959).

XIII

CASE HISTORIES

What signifies knowing the Names, if you know not the Natures of Things.—Benjamin Franklin.

*The midwife laid her hand on his thick skull,
With this prophetic blessing—Be thou dull.*
—John Dryden.

Because of my fear of seeming to assume the role of an omniscient schoolmaster lecturing moronic pupils, this chapter was nearly not written. But when discussing the idea of a chapter of case histories with other professional genealogists, I was so strongly urged to include one that I yielded. Let it be understood at the start that skilled genealogists are supposed to skip this chapter. Amateurs and professionals who lack experience in utilizing original record sources may perhaps find in it suggestions that will be helpful; and the general public, particularly that section of it which employs genealogists, may find it interesting to learn what record searching is like, and how professionals arrive at results. Of course I have had to draw these cases largely from my own experience in past searches, and I shall try to explain why each step of the way was taken. The case histories have no intrinsic value, aside from illustrating research methods.

I. Capt. Ebenezer Couch

The client had ascertained that her ancestor, Joel Bostwick Couch, was baptized 15 Apr. 1781 as son of Ebenezer Couch at the church in Washington, then Judea parish in Woodbury, Conn. From family sources she was certain that Ebenezer was a captain in the Revolutionary War, and that after the war he removed to Saratoga County, N. Y.

When she tried to join a Revolutionary society, it was discovered that years ago, at a time when this society had been lax in requiring full proofs, a descendant of another Ebenezer Couch, who lived in a different part of Connecticut and served as a private in the war, had joined the society and claimed for her ancestor all the services that appeared under the name of Ebenezer Couch, including the captain service which did not belong to him. My client's application had therefore been rejected, and to overthrow the false identification of the captain which had previously been accepted, it would now be necessary to trace the entire history of my client's Ebenezer with great thoroughness and to prove beyond possibility of doubt that he was the captain.

By consulting the three volumes in which muster rolls of Connecticut men in the Revolution are published, I ascertained that the residence of Captain Ebenezer Couch was stated as New Milford. This convinced me that my client was right in believing that the captain was her ancestor. The Ebenezer who served as private lived in a different section of the state, and it was unlikely that he would have been promoted from private to captain. Even in war time, things rarely happened that way. Again, the Ebenezer who had the son Joel Bostwick baptized at Washington was called of New Preston in the record. This was a parish located in the corner of three towns — New Milford, Kent, and the part of Woodbury which soon became Washington. I could therefore conclude that Capt. Ebenezer Couch lived in New Preston parish in the township of New Milford.

But my personal conclusions would not interest the client's society unless accompanied by evidence, and I had no proof that the Ebenezer who was father of Joel Bostwick was identical with the captain. To satisfy the requirements of the society, I should also have to ascertain Ebenezer's date of birth, and the names of his children.

There were two main Couch families in the state, and it seemed most probable, from my knowledge of migrations, that Captain Ebenezer belonged to the family which settled early at Fairfield. To obtain the vital records, two choices were possible. I could go to Fairfield and consult the original records, * or I could go to the State Library at Hartford and consult the Barbour Collection, which indexes all the town vital entries for the entire state. In this connection it should be explained that, if I had been writing a family history, or placing data in print, it would have been advisable to go to the town itself, and consult the original records; for, immensely useful as the Barbour copies are, they nevertheless contain numerous errors. By the time I had to make a decision, there were other considerations to take me to the State Library, so I went there.

The Fairfield records gave the birth of Ebenezer Couch, son of Ebenezer, on 20 Jan. 1733, which presumably was Old Style and meant 1733/4. His marriage and the births of some of his children were recorded in the vital records of Redding, a town which was a parish in Fairfield until it became a separate town in 1767. From this source I gleaned the following facts:

Ebenezer Couch, Jr., married Elizabeth "Carte" on 28 July 1761.
Children:

> John, born 5 May 1762
> Levi, born 25 Aug. 1763
> Anna, born 28 Feb. 1765
> Ebenezer, born 26 Feb. 1768
> Aaron, born 17 June 1772

The records of the Congregational Church in Redding are printed in the published history of that town, and the baptisms contained the

---

* The original early vital records of Fairfield, since then, have been deposited at the State Library.

following information:

John baptized 27 June 1762 as son of Ebenezer Couch, Jr.

Levi baptized 16 Oct. 1763 as son of *Lieut.* Ebenezer Couch.

Anne baptized 28 Apr. 1765 as dau. of Ebenezer and Elizabeth Couch.

Abner baptized 24 Mar. 1770 as son of Ebenezer and Elizabeth Couch.

(Abner died the day he was baptized.)

Aaron baptized 2 Aug. 1772 as son of Ebenezer Couch.

A fine copy of the church records of Greenfield parish in the town of Fairfield had been printed in The New England Historical and Genealogical Register, and under date of 27 July 1761 was entered the marriage of "Lt Ebenezer Couch of Reading" to "Elizabeth McCarty of Greenfield." Although the marriage occurred at Greenfield, it will be noted that the record was also found, with a discrepancy of a day, in the Redding town records.

In the marriage record, and in the baptismal record of one of the children, it should not be overlooked that Ebenezer was called Lieutenant. Since the great French and Indian War covered the period from 1755 to 1762, the next step was to consult the muster rolls of Connecticut men in that war, published in two fine volumes by the Connecticut Historical Society. These showed that Ebenezer Couch served as sergeant in the Campaign of 1757; and that he was commissioned ensign in 1758, being called "Ebenezer Couch, Jr." The printed Colonial records gave his commission as ensign in 1758, as second lieutenant in 1759, and as first lieutenant in 1760.

This military service was an important step in the identification of Ebenezer Couch, Jr., of Redding, with Captain Ebenezer Couch of New Milford. Men were not often commissioned captains for active service in the Revolutionary War without having had prior military experience and training. But a man who had shown the capacity to rise in rank in the French and Indian War from sergeant to first lieutenant would, if not too old for active service some fifteen years later, be eligible for promotion to a captaincy in the Revolutionary War.

How then to prove that Ebenezer Couch, Jr., of Redding, removed to New Milford? No mention of him was found subsequent to 1772 in the Redding records I had been able to consult. The land records of Redding, if consulted, might contain deeds given by Ebenezer after his removal, stating his new home as New Milford. However, I still had the problem of Ebenezer's second marriage and family to clear up, and as my expense account was quite limited, I thought it inadvisable to make a trip to Redding at that time, and eventually did not need to go there.

Marriages recorded in the parish records of New Preston Hill are printed in Bailey's Connecticut Marriages under the somewhat misleading heading of "Washington." Therein was found the marriage of Ebenezer Couch to Sarah Bostwick on 4 Nov. 1777. Study of a Bostwick genealogy and of a history of New Milford led to the theory that Sarah Bostwick was widow of a Joel Bostwick who died 11 Apr. 1777. Their family record was:

Joel Bostwick married Sarah Keeney on 21 June 1768.

Children:

CASE HISTORIES

Hannah, born 13 July 1769
Noble, born 28 Apr. 1771
Polly, born 12 Mar. 1773

It will be remembered that the client descended from Joel Bostwick Couch, son of Ebenezer by this second marriage to Sarah Bostwick, and it appeared likely that the son was named as a compliment
to the mother's former husband, a somewhat common practice at that
period, though it was even more common for a father to name a
daughter after his deceased former wife. Since Sarah's marriage to
Ebenezer occurred only a few months after the death of her first husband, it seemed likely that Ebenezer's name might occur in probate
records of Joel Bostwick's estate, and I hoped to find him referred to
as Captain, which very nearly would have established my line of proof.
New Milford was then in the Woodbury Probate District, but as
I did not want to incur the expense of a trip to Woodbury to consult the
record volumes, the files at the State Library were searched, and
showed that Ebenezer Couch, unfortunately not called by his military
title, had been appointed guardian to some of Joel Bostwick's young
children. A significant feature of the guardianship paper was that one
Daniel Copley signed Ebenezer's bond as surety. The name was already familiar to me, for I had obtained from my Danbury correspondent (Redding being then in the Danbury Probate District) an abstract of the will of Ebenezer's father, which proved that a sister of
Ebenezer Couch, Jr., of Redding was wife of Daniel Copley. It was
therefore a brother-in-law of Ebenezer Couch, Jr., who went on the
bond of Ebenezer Couch of New Milford — good circumstantial evidence for their identity.
In order to obtain further evidence, and to obtain a record of the
children of Ebenezer by his second marriage, a search was made of
records in the vicinity of New Milford. The following baptisms were
found in the New Preston Hill church records:

Hannah [child of] Joel Bostwick deceas'd [baptized] 30 Apr. 1780
Polly [child of] Joel Bostwick deceas'd [baptized] 30 Apr. 1780
Elizabeth [child of] Ebenezer Couch [baptized] 30 Apr. 1780
Joel Bostwick [child of] Ebenezer Couch [baptized] 15 Apr. 1781
Levi [child of] Ebenezer Couch [baptized] 22 June 1783
Caswell [child of] Ebenezer Couch [baptized] 14 Oct. 1785
Electa [child of] Ebenezer Couch [baptized] 15 June 1788

It grieved me to find that these church records failed to desig-
nate Ebenezer Couch in any of these entries or elsewhere by his
military title. However, it was interesting to note that Ebenezer
Couch had the two surviving Bostwick children baptized together with
his first child by his second wife, which provided further evidence
for her identity with Joel Bostwick's widow. It will be noted that the
baptism of Joel Bostwick Couch, which was recorded in Washington,
was found here also. Such duplications sometimes occur. This baptism was recorded both by the minister who performed it, and in the

register of the church to which the parents belonged.

More important evidence was found in the New Milford land records. New Preston being an outlying district, many of the residents there failed to have their family records entered, and the births of the children of Ebenezer Couch are hence not to be found. But the land records gave the following information. Ebenezer Couch of New Milford first bought land there in 1775 from Elias "Kinne" (note that Ebenezer's second wife was born a Kinney or Keeney). The land was located in New Preston. In 1780 Captain Ebenezer Couch bought land from Paul Welch, Jr.; and in 1783 Ebenezer Couch of New Milford, for love and affection, conveyed to his son John Couch part of the land "which I bought from Paul Welch" at New Preston. In 1791 John Couch deeded the same land back to "my father" Ebenezer Couch of the District of Ballston, Albany County, N. Y.

A careful comparison of the wording of the deeds shows conclusively that it was Captain Ebenezer Couch who had a son John and who removed to Ballston. It will be recalled that John, son of Ebenezer, Jr., was born at Redding in 1762, and hence was a few weeks over twenty-one years old when Captain Ebenezer conveyed to his son John. John remained in New Preston, and I found his gravestone inscription in a copy of New Preston inscriptions which some years before I had made from the stones. He died 12 June 1812, aged 50, which accords with the birth of John in Redding in 1762.

It now seemed to me that I had proved conclusively the identity of the Captain Ebenezer Couch of New Milford who served in the Revolutionary War. But the society would require his death record if obtainable, and the line of evidence was so involved that I feared it would be difficult to present it in a manner which would make it intelligible to the society genealogist. It was desirable to obtain Ebenezer's will if possible, so I wrote to the Clerk of the Surrogate's Court in Saratoga County, N. Y. It should here be pointed out to inexperienced amateurs that counties have been split up, hence the Ballston that was in Albany County in the 1791 deed is the same Ballston that today is in Saratoga County. Or perhaps not quite the same Ballston, for oftentimes towns also have been split up or have changed their bounds in some particulars.

During the course of the work, the 1790 census was of course consulted. Ebenezer Couch was listed as residing in "Ballstown," Albany County, and the next name under his was that of Daniel Couch. This fact had helped to confirm me in my original guess that Ebenezer of New Milford and Ballston was identical with Ebenezer, Jr., of Redding, for the latter had a brother Daniel.

But to return to the will, for I was lucky enough to obtain one. It was dated 17 Aug. 1800, with a codicil dated 16 Sept. 1800, and was proved 8 Nov. of the same year. The grand old soldier began with the words: I, Captain Ebenezer Couch, of Milton (Saratoga County); named his wife Sarah, oldest son John, sons Ebenezer, Jr., Aaron, Joel Bostwick, and "Levy," and daughters Anna, wife of Henry Whitlock, Elizabeth, wife of Benjamin Benedict, and Sarah K. Couch.

It will be seen that he called himself Captain, named his second wife, and named all his surviving children, both those recorded in Redding and those baptized in New Preston, and named in addition one later child, Sarah K. Couch, who was, we may surmise, given her mother's maiden name (Sarah Kinney). This last bit of evidence was so unexpectedly good that in reporting results it was possible to omit some of the earlier circumstantial evidence which had been rendered superfluous. Without the will, it would have required much additional time to arrange all the evidence in logical order and to explain it so intelligibly that it would bring conviction to a society genealogist.

It should always be remembered by genealogists that, however capable a society genealogist may be, the latter lacks a minute knowledge of record sources and conditions in the localities involved, and lacks also the advantage of having worked out a problem step by step. In preparing affidavits for the use of societies, everything should be clearly and logically presented, and all non-essential matter eliminated. Page references to printed sources, and certified copies of unpublished original records, should be furnished. The same remarks apply to reports made to clients, except that one need not go to the expense of obtaining certified copies unless the client prefers it.

II. Rev. Nathaniel Brewster

This is a problem I studied chiefly for my own amusement, and since I was unable to give sufficient time and money to the research, it remains not positively solved.

As long ago as 1860, Savage in his Genealogical Dictionary of New England stated that Rev. Nathaniel Brewster, one of the first graduates of Harvard, was probably son of Francis Brewster of New Haven, Conn. Despite this shrewd suggestion, most descendants and most printed accounts have tried, and still are trying, to find a place for Nathaniel in the family of Elder William Brewster of the Mayflower.

It is a mystery why Americans of colonial descent should be so obsessed to trace their ancestry to one of the Mayflower passengers. Great as was the role played by the coming of the Mayflower, it has been overemphasized, and unquestionably just as good people came on later ships. Only a handful of the Mayflower passengers left descendants, and these for several generations lived chiefly in certain localities. This makes it difficult for those whose ancestors lived chiefly in other localities to achieve a Mayflower descent, but perhaps the very difficulty of it adds zest to the search. At any rate, it is true that nearly everyone with a Cooke, Rogers, Brewster or other line where the surname was identical with that of a Mayflower passenger, assumes identity of family, and many cling to such beliefs even when their theories have been definitely disproved. Hence it is easy to understand why descendants of Rev. Nathaniel Brewster are so reluctant to relinquish a Mayflower claim which many hit-or-miss genealogists of the past accepted and misled their clients into believing.

Suppose then a genealogist today is commissioned to ascertain the parentage of Nathaniel: how will he go about it?

He will consult the Brewster Genealogy and discover that the compiler found no place for Nathaniel in the family of Elder William; but relegated Nathaniel and some mention of his family to the appendix. He will write to officials of the Mayflower Society and learn that descendants of Rev. Nathaniel Brewster are not accepted as descendants of the Elder. He will study the known family of Elder William for himself, and fail to find valid evidence, or even sound genealogical reasons, for placing Nathaniel in that family.

He will note the suggestion of Savage that Nathaniel was probably son of Francis Brewster of New Haven, Conn., and consider it worth while to pursue it and discover, if possible, what facts led Savage to this theory.

Francis Brewster was a well-to-do merchant and was dignified with the prefix of respect ("Mr.") which at that period was applied only to men of birth and breeding. His social status was therefore consonant with the education of a son at college. The printed records of New Haven Colony, in the list of heads and estates that belongs probably to the year 1641, give him a family of nine persons. These records also refer by name to a youthful son Joseph. After Mr. Brewster was lost in the "Phantom Ship" in 1646, the colonial records show that his widow Lucy married Dr. Thomas Pell, who was also a man of good social position, having a brother in England who was a doctor of divinity. With her second husband, she removed by 1650 to Fairfield, and she and her daughters Elizabeth and Mary Brewster were among the witnesses in the noted Staples slander suit.

Joseph, Elizabeth and Mary are all of the Brewster children whose names have as yet been rescued from oblivion. It is very unfortunate that few wills of the period when Mr. Francis Brewster died have been preserved in New Haven. Dr. Pell and his wife disposed of the New Haven realty, hence there are not conveyances from the children who should have been the eventual heirs. At a later period, the legality of a transfer by the widow and her second husband would have been questionable, and confirmatory quitclaims from the children would be likely to appear. As a matter of fact, a much later deed, which I long overlooked, was given after the Rev. Nathaniel Brewster's death by his eldest son in Brookhaven, Long Island, apparently in confirmation of the Pell sale.

All the children of Mr. Brewster seem to have been born before New Haven was founded, hence the church records, which begin very early, do not contain baptisms of the Brewster children. All the cards seem to have been stacked against us so far as New Haven records are concerned, so we journey now to Fairfield.

Here conditions are almost worse, for there are no very early vital or church records preserved. Fortunately, Dr. Pell survived until 1669, and his will, because of his large land interests in both places, is recorded both in Fairfield and in New York State. To it we turn for clues.

After mentioning that "God has taken to himself my beloved wife Luzy," he provided that the children of his brother in England should inherit his lands, and a nephew did come to America and settle in Westchester County on a part of the landed estate. Valuable legacies of silverware and horses were given to Daniel Burr and Abigail Burr his wife; and others who were mentioned or given smaller legacies were "my son French," Nathaniel French, Elizabeth White, Mary White, and Nathaniel White. After providing for servants, and forgiving four poor men their debts to him, he appointed Daniol Burr and John Banks executors of the will.

From the reference to his wife Lucy it may be surmised that she died not very long before the will was written. It is also clear that his own nearest relatives were in England, and the will explicitly states that he had been "denied natural issue of his body." We know from the colonial records alluded to above that his wife's daughters Elizabeth and Mary Brewster had been living in his household in 1654. We do not know what became of the older Brewster children, and it is possible that some of them returned to England to inherit property after their father's death. But these younger children who as girls had been brought into his home would very likely have won the affection of the childless physician.

The "son French" could hardly have been other than husband of one of the Brewster stepdaughters. If we suppose that one of the Brewster girls married a French and was mother of the Nathaniel French named in Dr. Pell's will, and that the other married a White and was mother of Elizabeth, Mary, and Nathaniel White, we have accounted for most of those named in the will, as the little children of favorite stepdaughters. The Whites have been located in Westchester County, where Dr. Pell had large land holdings and spent part of his time. The Frenches I have not located, but would be inclined to look for in Westchester County, on Long Island, or possibly in New Jersey.

Notice that the known Brewster girls were named Elizabeth and Mary, and that these were also the names of the two White girls. The Whites had a son Nathaniel, as did also the Frenches. This is a significant point. It was a distinction to have a college graduate and clergyman in a family, and if Rev. Nathaniel Brewster was son of Francis, then two of his sisters named a son for him.

Coming now to the Burrs, the marriage of Daniel Burr to Abigail Brewster is found recorded at Stamford. The will of Rev. Nathaniel Brewster, which is in print, remembered his grandchildren Daniel and Abigail Burr. Abigail (Brewster) Burr had died, leaving these two children. In other words, if Rev. Nathaniel was son of Francis, then Abigail the wife of Daniel Burr was granddaughter of Dr. Pell's wife Lucy; and she was the only member of the Brewster family living at Fairfield at the time of Dr. Pell's death. Abigail, after her grandmother's death, may have shown kindly attentions to her old stepgrandfather, and the best bed and silver spoons he left her may have belonged to her grandmother. Abigail's husband may have looked after some of the doctor's business interests, which would explain the legacy to him of all the doctor's horses (excepting mares) both in New England and in New York. It would also explain his being made an executor of the will. The other executor, John Banks, was a magistrate and one of the most prominent citizens of Fairfield, and his appointment was probably to balance that of Daniel Burr, and to make sure that the interests of Dr. Pell's own relatives in England were properly looked after.

Much of this is theory, yes; but it is theory which fits and explains all the known facts. Legacies meant something in 1669; they were not often the outgrowth of whim or mere fancy.

The next step is to study the career of Rev. Nathaniel Brewster and see whether it offers any confirmatory evidence. Born probably not later than 1618, Nathaniel was graduated from Harvard in 1642, which would indicate that he started his college course not long after New Haven was settled. The Civil War broke out in England about this time, and he returned there, remaining as long as the Puritans were in control. After the Restoration, he came back to New England.

It has been stated that in 1649 he appeared in Walderwich, Suffolk County, England, as attorney for Thomas Pell. I have not verified this statement, but there is no reason to question it. What connection had he with Dr. Pell if not his stepson? Again, in 1655 he went to Ireland, and not long after married a daughter of Roger Ludlow who was then living in Dublin. Ludlow had been the founder of Fairfield and its most prominent citizen while he remained there; he must have been well acquainted with Dr. Pell, who was of his own social class, a class not numerous in New England. Nathaniel, if Pell's stepson, could have carried a letter to Mr. Ludlow when he went to Ireland. Doubtless, there were other ways he could have met him, but again, the theory fits.

Upon his return to America in 1663, Nathaniel, after preaching a short period in Boston, preached in Eastchester, N.Y. Was this through the influence of Dr. Pell, a large landholder there? Be that as it may, in 1665, when the church in New London, Conn., voted to give Mr. Brewser a "call," it was also voted to request Mr. Pell to use his influence. Mr. Pell had married the widow of Francis Brewster, and what influence did he have over Nathaniel Brewster unless the latter were his stepson?

Dr. Pell until the time of his death runs like a motif through the career of Rev. Nathaniel Brewster, who eventually settled in Setauket, Brookhaven township, Long Island, and remained there until his own death. One of his grandchildren was named Francis Brewster.

Unless something turns up unexpectedly, not much more that is obvious suggests itself in the line of research on this side of the Atlantic. The next step would be to have research done abroad. Most, if not all, of the children of Francis Brewster were born on the other side, and if the baptism of his son Nathaniel should be found in an English parish, our case would be impregnable. Even though the present evidence is entirely circumstantial, so much evidence from different sources all pointing to the same conclusion is too much to explain away as mere coincidence. It is here a matter of the correct interpretation of the evidence, and the trained genealogist is better qualified than amateurs of comparatively slight experience to interpret the known facts and to draw legitimate deductions from them.

Note: The foregoing account has been left virtually as it was written in 1930, to show how circumstantial evidence can be used to build a strong case for reaching conclusions. The conclusion that the Rev. Nathaniel Brewster was son of Francis has since been proved by

CASE HISTORIES

English records, and the evidence has been published elsewhere.

III. Capt. John Gill

The problem was to determine the parentage of Capt. John Gill, who lived and died in a region close to the boundary line between the towns of North Haven and Hamden, Conn. Since both of these towns were originally parts of New Haven, we should have looked for his ancestry here, were it not for the fact that at the time of his birth no family of the name lived in New Haven; on the other hand, research in other Connecticut towns where Gill families lived failed to provide a parentage for this John Gill.

The gravestone of John Gill stated that he died 10 May 1807, aged 83, and this would place the year of his birth as approximately 1724.

Although he had eleven children, their names did not seem particularly significant, except that the eldest son was named Ebenezer Mansfield Gill. This escaped attention at first, because the mother of John's wife was born a Mansfield, so it was assumed that the name came from her side. But as a last desperate measure, the will of one Ebenezer Mansfield was consulted, and it was found that he gave a legacy to "John Potter alias Gill" whom he had brought up. The alias suggested the probable solution, for the experienced genealogist knows that its use at that period very often implies illegitimacy.

Since Potters were a New Haven family, and Gills were not, it seemed most likely that John's father was a Gill and his mother a Potter. The same conclusion was hinted by the fact that John himself employed the name Gill throughout his life, for it was then the usual custom for a child born out of wedlock to assume the name of the reputed father rather than the mother's surname. The next step, then, was to search the County Court records and files for a Potter bastardy case in or near 1724. It was found that one Sarah Potter was before the Court in 1724 on such a charge, and accused one Thomas Gill, transient of New Haven, of the paternity of her child. A study of the Potter and Mansfield family trees revealed the fact that Sarah Potter was a younger first cousin of the Ebenezer Mansfield whose will proves that he brought up "John Potter alias Gill."

The case could now be considered genealogically proved; but as a final step the records of the New Haven First Church were consulted. In 1728 the baptism of John, son of Sarah Potter, was entered. At that period in these church records the names of the infants baptized, but not the names of their parents, were stated. But as the minister may have felt some doubt as to the surname which should be given to John, he compromised by adding the mother's name.

John Gill became a respected citizen and the progenitor of a respectable family. He rose through the usual grades of ensign and lieutenant to a captaincy in the local militia.

This example is given because occasionally the solution of a peculiarly knotty problem proves to have been illegitimacy. Rarely can such a problem be solved except by a most thorough examination and study of original sources; and rarely is the line of proof so complete as in the example.

IV. Hannah Merrill

The problem was to discover the parentage of Hannah Merrill who married Ebenezer Griswold at Norwich, Conn., on 7 Nov. 1748. The Griswolds were a Norwich family; except for a few scattering entries, the Merrills were not.

The main Connecticut family of Merrills was founded by a son of the first Nathaniel Merrill of Newbury, Mass., who came early to Hartford, Conn., and had several sons. A study of this family was made, the wills in Manwaring's Digest of Hartford Probate Records aiding in the process of elimination. It was found that only one Hannah existed in the Hartford family early enough for the marriage in 1748. She was daughter of an Ebenezer Merrill and was baptized in West Hartford in 1728. "A Merrill Memorial" did indeed state that this was the Hannah who married Ebenezer Griswold, but no record source was quoted, and there was no reason to suppose that the statement was more than a guess. Ebenezer Merrill removed with his family to New Hartford, which is in a different part of the State from Norwich, and on the face of it, the probabilities were against this Hannah marrying in Norwich. Also, Ebenezer Merrill's family did not account for other stray Merrills who appeared in Norwich about the time of Hannah's marriage there.

The probate files in the State Library did not contain the estate of Ebenezer Merrill, and the genealogist decided it would be a waste of time to visit New Hartford.

Another family of Merrills had been located who lived much nearer Norwich and were not accounted for in "A Merrill Memorial," and attention was turned to this family. The first was a Thomas Merrill who settled in Saybrook as early as the 1680's and had five sons. As the wife of Thomas was named Hannah, it seemed probable that this name would reappear among his grandchildren. Research in vital, probate and land records proved that the eldest son remained in Saybrook and had no issue; another settled in Hebron and had no daughter Hannah; a third settled in New London (close to Norwich) and had a daughter Hannah, but probate records proved that she married a Nettleton; the other two sons settled in Killingworth. One of them had a daughter Hannah, born in 1728, and no marriage was found for her. This Hannah's father had no probate record, but in his old age conveyed his lands to his sons. The daughters had doubtless received their portions in movables during his lifetime, hence there was nothing to show whether this Hannah married Ebenezer Griswold or another, or even whether she lived to marry.

As between the Hannah whose father settled in New Hartford and the one born in Killingworth, both born 1728, chances would favor the latter, because Killingworth was much nearer Norwich and there was considerable intercourse between the families of the two places. But the other stray Merrills in Norwich records were not accounted for in the Killingworth family any better than they had been in the Hartford family, so the genealogist decided to look further.

Who were the Merrills who appeared in Norwich? This was of importance, for it led to the solution of the problem. In addition to

Hannah who married Ebenezer Griswold on 7 Nov. 1748, there was Susanna who married Elisha Griswold on 8 Nov. 1748, just one day later. These two marriages, with the births of the children of each, were recorded on the same page of the original record book. Ebenezer and Elisha Griswold were brothers, and as they practically had a double wedding and both married Merrill girls, it was natural to guess that the latter might have been sisters. There was also an Elizabeth Merrill who married Moses Hazen on 13 Nov. 1755, and the entry called her "of Norwich," indicating the probability that her father lived in Norwich.

The only male Merrill who appeared in Norwich vital records at that time was a Peter Merrill with wife Mary, who had a son Jedediah born in 1740, and a daughter Ruth born in 1742.

It took very little figuring to prove that Hannah, Susanna and Elizabeth could have been older children of Peter, born before he came to Norwich, if Jedediah and Ruth were his youngest children. Furthermore, Hannah (Merrill) Griswold gave the names Jedediah and Ruth to two of her children.

The name Peter was common in the branches of the Massachusetts family which remained in the vicinity of Newbury. "A Merrill Memorial" showed that one Peter settled in Haverhill, Mass., and married 24 Jan. 1721/2, Mary Haseltine. The births of four children were given, which were verified in the printed records of Haverhill. These were Mary in 1723, Susanna in 1725, Hannah in 1727, and Joseph in 1730. The latter book added the baptisms of two more children: Elizabeth in 1735, and Mary in 1737. The death of the first Mary was found.

Any genealogist capable of weighing evidence would now conclude that the problem was solved. Peter and Mary Merrill disappeared from Haverhill records just three years before their appearance in Norwich. No other Peter with wife Mary could be identified with the Norwich Peter and Mary. The Haverhill couple had daughters Susanna, Hannah, and Elizabeth, who would have been brought to Norwich with them; and each one of these three girls was born at just the right time to be available for the marriages of Susanna, Hannah and Elizabeth recorded in Norwich. Then there were the names Jedediah and Ruth which Peter gave to two children, and which Hannah also gave to two of hers.

While this did not constitute legal proof, yet after a survey of the entire Merrill family in both Massachusetts and Connecticut had been made down to this period, these correspondences could not be explained away as coincidental. Three unrelated Merrill girls did not stray into Norwich all by themselves; things did not happen that way. They were brought there by their parents; and the only male Merrill who had made his home in Norwich was the very Peter who had three daughters of the right names and ages.

However, because the incorrect identification of Hannah had been given circulation in "A Merrill Memorial," it was desirable to obtain legal evidence if possible. A search was made, and Peter had no estate probated in the Norwich district, where it should have been if he died in Norwich. The land records were searched and it was found that Peter bought a house in Norwich in 1747, which he sold in 1755; the same year, he bought another house, and he appeared no more in Norwich records. The second house was sold by Jedediah Merrill of Norwich in 1763. Jedediah's deed failed to recite how he acquired title; perhaps by an unrecorded deed. Otherwise, we must assume that Peter removed and died elsewhere, to explain the lack of probation of his estate in the Norwich district.

The deeds showed that the land was in New Concord parish, which later became the town of Bozrah. This place was visited, for a search of church and land records, but nothing about Merrills was found.

In the 1790 Census, Jedediah Merrill is found in Vermont. This was probably the son of Peter, since Jedediah of Vermont is not accounted for in "A Merrill Memorial." The Griswolds also moved to Vermont, which increases the likelihood of this conclusion. Did Peter move to Vermont in advance of his son, die there, and will him the Norwich house and lot? These clues might have been followed, but the case was conclusive enough without adding the expense of a Vermont search, which might have proved disappointing if undertaken.

Note: The above evidence and conclusions were submitted to Mr. Samuel Merrill, the compiler of "A Merrill Memorial," and accepted by him, with the explanation that he did not do the research in Connecticut personally and had relied on material furnished by others in his identification of Hannah. This case is a good illustration of the risk involved in too readily accepting printed statements for which no evidence is set forth.

V. Shadrach Potter

Our final case history will show briefly how special knowledge is often a great aid in the proper handling of printed sources.

A lady came into an historical society library, where the librarian chanced to be a skilled genealogist. She was shown the location of books on Rhode Island genealogy, and worked for several days with them. As she seemed discouraged, the librarian asked if she could help her. She was looking, she said, for a Shadrach Potter, but had been unable to locate him. The librarian said: "Perhaps we shall find Meshech and Abednego Potter"; and sure enough, Meshech and Abednego were found in the 1790 Census, and through their residence Shadrach was located.

Knowledge of Bible nomenclature solved this problem, for it will be recalled that these three individuals were mentioned together in the Book of Daniel, and the Potter father had conferred on sons all three of these unusual names. The helpful librarian was Ethel Lord Scofield, a genealogist of the old school.

XIV

HOW TO COMPILE A FAMILY HISTORY

The Moving Finger writes; and, having writ,
Moves on; nor all your Piety nor Wit
Shall lure it back to cancel half a Line,
Nor all your Tears wash out a Word of it.
— *Omar Khayyám.*

Out of the cradle endlessly rocking, ...
I, chanter of pains and joys, uniter of here and hereafter, . . .
A reminiscence sing.
— *Walt Whitman.*

If it is desired to trace the origin of the family in England, a specialist in English research should be retained. One without experience can but rarely achieve the best results by attempting to handle this part of the work personally; though if American records contain strong clues as to the English place of origin, a novice can sometimes make a good beginning by writing to rectors for entries in parish registers and by having wills abstracted. If the American progenitor is traced in England, a full copy of the English records obtained should be printed, not merely the compiler's conclusions based on them. A coat-of-arms should not be used as an illustration unless proof of descent from the armigerous family is offered.

Records in and near the town where the family made its first permanent American home should be thoroughly searched. If the compiler has never worked in contemporary record sources of the Seventeenth and Eighteenth Centuries, it will take him a long time to familiarize himself with the script of the period, the classes of records which are available, and the correct interpretation of the records pertaining to his family. It is sometimes said of a man who insists on acting as his own lawyer that he has a fool for a client; and too often the same observation is appropriate for a man who insists on being his own genealogist. But while an overwhelming majority of family histories written by amateurs are inferior productions, there are notable exceptions, and some of the best family histories to be found on library shelves were compiled by amateurs. It is to be noted, however, that these exceptions were compiled by persons who in addition to the required type of mentality had enjoyed the advantages of superior education, and who either possessed independent means or had the support of a family association, enabling them to devote their whole time for several years to the work.

For the writing of a family history, if it is to be accurate and anywhere near complete, is no light undertaking. It should if possible be compiled entirely by one person, whether that person be the financial backer of the work or the professional genealogist employed by him, for it is very difficult for a second worker to take over a half-completed compilation, with its infinite mass of detail, and complete it. This of course does not apply to employing other searchers from time to time to cover specific records in places which the compiler is unable to visit personally.

The individual members of the family should not be assigned reference numbers until the last minute before publication. If they are assigned earlier, they will certainly have to be changed, for up to the last minute new material will be found affecting the numbering system. There is one system which can be employed from the start, but aside from this advantage it is inferior to the systems in more general use and is not to be recommended. Of course, temporary numbering can be adopted, but is likely to cause confusion. A better plan is to index the individuals as the work progresses. A card index is the most satisfactory, and each card should contain the name of the individual, his year date of birth, and perhaps his chief place of residence when that is known, together of course with the reference to the page of the manuscript where information about him will be found.

Another good plan is to chart the early generations for quick reference, so as to be able to see at a glance the place occupied by each individual in the family. But even with these aids, a good memory is an almost indispensable asset in handling and arranging the material expeditiously.

When the book is in type, an index must be compiled as rapidly as possible. It used to be the fashion to have several indices, one for male descendants bearing the family name, one for female descendants born with the family name, one for husbands of daughters, one for wives of sons, and so on. It is much simpler and better for those who use the book to get everything into a single index. It is useful if the year date of birth is added to every individual who was born with the family name, or something equally distinguishing added, for it is appalling to have to look up a hundred page references if such names as John or Mary are sought.

Some histories, excellent ones among them, split a family into branches, taking up the descendants of each son or grandson of the first settler in order. This is very annoying to anyone who is interested in the early generations of the family and who has to consult each separate section of the book to locate all the great-grandchildren of the settler. Start with the settler, then come to the second generation and carry down each of his children or sons at least, then give the entire third generation, and follow this system down to the present.

Never attempt to trace descendants in female lines beyond the children of daughters. It is impossible to do so completely, as will be explained in the chapter entitled "Growth of an American Family." A large percentage of errors in the better family histories are in the female line, where the compiler's knowledge was less encyclopaedic. Theoretically each family name should have its own history, and sooner or later, if the present interest continues, each of them will have. Most of the female lines found in the histories that pretend to give descendants on all lines, male or female, are "lifted" from other family histories, while those not found already in print are usually omitted. It adds nothing to the sum of genealogical knowledge to keep reprinting matter that has already been published in adequate form, and if inaccurate, the new compiler is compounding the errors of his predecessors.

When the genealogist has made a good beginning towards the arrangement of the first six generations — of course on some branches he will have acquired considerable later data — he should pick out all services in colonial wars and in the Revolution from printed muster rolls, and should have abstracts made of all Revolutionary pension files at Washington, pertaining to the family name. The difficulties are great if there were several early families of the same surname, when the compiler is interested in but one of these families. Sooner or later, he will have to write a partial history of the other families as well, to avoid confusion and to make sure of keeping them distinct from the family he is compiling.

Land records of the localities where the early generations lived are helpful in tracing individuals who removed to new localities, as their new homes are specified in their conveyances if they sold property subsequent to removal. The great dispersion took place in the decades following the Revolutionary War, and families moved from one pioneer settlement to another until they scattered throughout the entire country. The census records in Washington are a great aid in tracing migratory branches during the period when the eastern reservoirs of human stock were sending wave after wave of pioneer families to all the western lands.

It would be a hopeless task to attempt to search the public records of every locality where members of your family ever resided. After you have brought most of the branches down to about 1800, begin soliciting information from descendants. Do not begin to do this earlier, because interested descendants who send records for inclusion will write to you periodically to inquire when the book will be published, or to find out why it has not been published yet, and you do not want this annoyance to start sooner than need be.

You can secure addresses from city directories and telephone directories, and if these are not accessible to you for the whole country, advertising agencies for a fee will prepare lists of addresses. The city cousin, when he replies, can give you the address of the country cousin.

Various printed forms have been devised for the use of compilers in obtaining data from descendants. All of the forms have some good features, but no one type is perfect. In fact, I dare assert that a perfect form is impossible to devise. If too simple, incomplete information will be received; whereas, if the form provides for every contingency, it becomes so complicated and appears so formidable to the recipient that the compiler may consider himself lucky if it comes back filled out at all.

It is well to have a neat circular printed, announcing the preparation of the genealogy, and requesting data of the recipient's branch.

It should specify in words of one syllable just what kind of information is desired. If any blank form accompanies the circular, in my judgment a simple form is to be preferred. Well educated people are weary of questionnaires; poorly educated people are afraid of showing ignorance by filling them out incorrectly; and both classes are prone to postpone and neglect what is for them a tedious task. Certainly at times one gets better results by allowing the descendants to write out the information in their own way. If incomplete an exchange of two or three letters should make good the defects of the first reply.

The printed circulars should bring at least one reply for every eight or ten sent out. After a month, a personal letter, signed even if it be a mimeographed form letter, should be mailed to those who have not responded. This may bring more results than the circular brought: the personal touch does count. A third and final appeal should follow after another month has passed, asking for addresses of interested relatives if the recipient himself is positively not interested.

Self-addressed envelopes should always be enclosed, but it is wasteful to stamp them. Those who are interested enough to send data will not be deterred by the lack of postage, while the stamp will have no influence on those who are not interested.

If the descendants who send data ask for information in return, give it to them. Don't tell them to wait and buy a copy of the book. Some of the elderly ones will not live to see the publication. Remember that these people are doing you a favor. They fail to realize what an added burden it places on the overworked compiler when they ask him where the family originated, or their line of descent, or whether an ancestor served in the Revolution. But neither do you realize what a nuisance it is to them to look up their records or write to cousins to obtain more information for you. Perhaps they are as overworked as you are. A generous attitude on the part of the compiler will not affect the sale of the book, and it is only decent to show consideration to these voluntary contributors.

Writers of family histories too often waste pages extolling the virtues of their family, or telling what special traits distinguish it. There is no such thing, when dealing with ten generations and thousands of individuals, as a good family or a bad family. The new strains brought in by the wives in each generation must impart a tendency upward or downward to the succeeding generations. Every family has its distinguished members and branches, and its less reputable members and branches.

The branches that achieve distinction are prominent, and the compiler usually has little difficulty in obtaining their records. If a branch sinks too low in the social scale, it drops out of sight, and you fail to secure records from its members. They are not proud of themselves, so they are not proud of their family, and if your circulars reach them, they rarely reply. Hence most genealogies enlarge the achievements of the best part of the family, and neglect the worst part; and most compilers are satisfied with this result, even if they have made an honest effort to have all branches fully represented.

As for the prevalent notion that certain traits characterize a certain American family, it is sheer nonsense. It may well be that a dominant trait shows itself here and there in some lines over the course of several generations. But the law of averages and the laws of heredity preclude the possibility that all, or even a majority, of the several thousand descendants of the first American ancestor will inherit one certain trait. And this is considering only descendants in the male line. Or look at the question from a different angle. Suppose that a living member of your family numbers among his ancestors from five hundred to a thousand immigrant ancestors — and that is a fair computation if he is wholly of early colonial ancestry: what are his chances of inheriting a given trait from a single one of these forbears, even though that one be his ancestor on the male line?

Yet even exceptionally intelligent people show a lack of reflection on this subject. When I was compiling a genealogy, many descendants who had believed that the first settler was a French Huguenot were naturally somewhat incredulous when his parentage was discovered in England. One of them sent me a charming picture of an ancestor on this line, who was in the sixth generation of descent from the first settler, and pointed out his dark, handsome, French-looking features. I had to admit it; he did look French. Yet the subject of this portrait had thirty-two ancestors in the same generation with the first settler on the male line, and since he could have inherited his physical traits from any one of these ancestors or from any combination of them, the chances were thirty-one to one against close resemblance to the male-line ancestor. In find, this sort of evidence is not competent to decide a question of this sort.

To summarize: Be sure to make or procure thorough search of original record sources for the early generations of your family; go through all the printed sources in a large library if possible, for many valuable items will be gleaned in this way, particularly pertaining to the later generations; collect all you can from living descendants; and index your book adequately. The sale of the book may refund actual printing costs unless a de luxe style of paper, printing, binding, and illustrating is desired. The cost of the research and of the compilation, or your own time if you did this work personally, is your contribution to the family history. No genealogy published today, if the work has been properly and thoroughly done, can produce a monetary profit.

In selecting a printer, a firm that specializes in genealogical printing can offer the compiler greater facilities and take more burdens off his shoulders than one that is inexperienced in this field. The compiler should learn the most common printing symbols, such as underlining once for italics and twice for small capitals, and employ them for the convenience of the compositors. Untrained compilers add much to printing costs by failing to give detailed instructions at the start, necessitating changes after type has been set. A page on which the matter concerning heads of families is set in ten-point type, that concerning children in eight-point type, and footnotes in six-point, makes an attractive appearance.

When your genealogy is going through the press, you will receive first a galley-proof, which should be read and corrected with the greatest care. If changes or additions have to be made, be sure to attend to them at this stage, because if made after the book is paged, they will prove more costly. The page-proof should require only checking to see that the changes have been made. Always read the <u>whole line</u> in which a change, however slight, was made; for in lino-type printing the whole line is removed and a new one set, and in correcting one error a different one may have been made. If an in-sertion in one line has made necessary the resetting of several sub-sequent lines, perhaps to the end of the paragraph, do not overlook them, for although they may have been correct in the galley-proof, there may be mistakes in them now.

Many genealogies are issued in parts. This scheme has found general favor because the cost of printing a cloth-bound volume of, let us say, a thousand pages, is so great that the resulting price of a single copy will be prohibitive to many descendants and will reduce sales to a minimum. By issuing the genealogy in from three to six parts, bound in heavy paper, a moderate price can be asked for each part, and for the purchaser the cost of the whole publication will be spread over a long period, say from two to five years. This plan also gives the compiler more time to collect material on the later genera-tions, and to correct any errors that have been discovered in the earlier parts.

Printing by offset is now much employed because it is much cheaper than letterpress. However, the preparation of master copy is a chore, and mistakes are often hard to rectify. The employment of an expert to type the master copy dilutes the saving obtained from offset printing.

Do not make the costly mistake of printing too large an edition. Two hundred copies are enough, and often more than enough, for a pedigree book giving the compiler's ancestry on various lines. For the usual type of family history, an edition of from three to four hun-dred copies should suffice. The higher the price asked per copy, the fewer are the sales, and the size of the edition should be limited ac-cordingly.

In printing copies of, or quotations from, original records, it is questionable whether much is gained by following the spelling and punctuation of the original. To be sure, there is a scholarly satis-faction in making verbatim copies, exact in every detail, and it should always be done in printing volumes of vital or church records. But in a family history, which is to be distributed among descendants who for the most part are not accustomed to the vagaries of the ancient scribes, modern spelling would better convey the meaning of a tran-scription. Undoubtedly, many readers are bewildered by verbatim copies, smile perhaps at their quaintness, and pass them by unread.

It is very nearly impossible to place in print an exact copy of any old hand-written record. There were abbreviations and symbols not to be found in the fonts of modern printers. The confusion of 'u' and 'v' is not a real difference in spelling, since these letters were con-sidered identical, and the same observation applies to the use of the capital 'J' for 'I'. Just why the use of the initial 'ff' in place of 'F', and of the long 's', should be preserved in modern printed copies, while no attempt is made to preserve the old form of the letters 'r' and 'd', the old capital 'C', or the 'e' that was formed like an 'o' looped at the top, is a complete mystery. All of these belong in the same category and were differences in writing the letters, not real differences in spelling. If an exact reproduction is sought, a photostatic copy instead of a printed one should be found more satisfactory. Or perhaps I should have said, more unsatisfactory, since many of the readers would be unable to read the photostatic copy at all, while they can struggle through the so-called verbatim printed copy after a fashion.

It might also be pointed out that two experts would rarely make an identical transcription of an old record. Take a single example. Where a certain letter was shaped the same way, only size indicates whether it was intended as a small or capital letter. The careless scribe sometimes employed an intermediate size, which one expert might read as small, another expert as large. But in printing, an intermediate size would be impractical, so the copyist can only toss a coin to decide whether one of these uncertain letters should be set upper or lower case.

My personal opinion is that, for family histories, modernized spelling for everything except personal names should be adopted. Should it not be the function of the expert antiquarian to dress the records of the past in the style that will make them most attractive to the general reading public? If it be pointed out that I have not always backed this opinion by my personal practice, I can only plead the strength of precedent. The genealogical profession, like the legal, has its precedents; and both professions should be less reluctant than they are to abandon precedents which, if ever useful, are so no longer.

Your finished book will be a pride and joy to you forever; and the praise of it, sweet music to your ears. Yet be not surprised if the harmony admits discordant notes. The man who failed to answer your impassioned pleas for information may criticise the book because his branch was omitted. And if an overlooked typographical error records one of the prominent descendants as marrying the mother of his child a month or so after that child's date of birth — well, a few florist bills for your friends to pay is the worst that can befall.

He that can compose himself, is wiser than he that composes books.
                                                        —Benjamin Franklin.

XV

GROWTH OF A COLONIAL FAMILY

*And God blessed them, and God said unto them, Be fruitful, and
multiply, and replenish the earth, and subdue it.—Genesis.*

> *One family— ......*
> *Part of the host have crossed the flood*
> *And part are crossing now.*
> *—Charles Wesley.*

The rapidity with which the descendants of early settlers in New
England increased has been frequently commented upon, but actual
statistics for the first one hundred and fifty years are difficult to obtain and are for the most part estimates. To check these estimates,
it will be illuminating to set forth the actual increase among the descendants of an early immigrant.

For the purpose of this study the family of John and Tabitha
Thomas of New Haven, Conn., has been selected. In making a choice
it seemed advisable, with the object of saving unnecessary labor, to
select a family and a locality with which I was thoroughly familiar.
Care was also taken to select an immigrant whose children and grandchildren remained near the place of the birth; otherwise it might have
proved impossible to trace the descendants completely enough to make
the study of statistical value. Finally it seemed unfair to select an
immigrant who had but two or three children, or one who had twelve
or fourteen children. John Thomas had seven children, and his family
fulfilled the other requirements.

John and Tabitha Thomas were born, presumably, about 1615,
and came to New England shortly before 1640, when the wave of immigration from England was nearing its crest. They had, as has been
stated, seven children, all of whom lived to marry and have issue.
From the seven children sprang, in the third generation, 49 grandchildren, or an average of 7 children in each family.

Of these 49 grandchildren, 8 died under 20 years of age, 4 died
unmarried aged above 20 years, 1 married but died childless, and
the remaining 36 produced between them, 230 individuals in the fourth
generation, or an average of a trifle less than 6-1/2 children in each
family. These 230 individuals are believed to include all of the surviving great-grandchildren of John Thomas, but there may have been
a few unrecorded children who died in infancy. In several instances
in this and in the succeeding (fifth) generation, the names of surviving
children have been ascertained from probate records, when no record of births or baptisms could be found. Therefore the number of
children born should be increased slightly in the fourth generation and

considerably in the fifth generation, in order to include such unrecorded children as presumably died young.

Of the 230 great-grandchildren, 22 died under 20 years of age, 9 died unmarried aged above 20 years, 6 married but died childless,* the fate of 27 is unknown, and the remaining 166 produced 993 known individuals in the fifth generation, or an average of a trifle less than 6 children in each family. Of these 993 known individuals, 33 were doubly descended from John Thomas, being the children of cousins. This number should be increased, to allow for the progeny of the 27 members of the fourth generation whose fate is unknown. About half of them are known to have reached maturity, and several of them are known to have married; if we suppose that even 10 of the 27 had 6 children apiece, we increase our figures by 60, making 1,053. But in the case of 166 known parents of the fourth generation, there is reason to believe that a few of them left more children than have been located, and unquestionably there were a number of unrecorded children who died young. In view of all these considerations, it is conservative to estimate that John and Tabitha Thomas had close to 1,100 great-great-grandchildren, of whom 993 individuals have been definitely traced.

Before we consider the bearing of these figures on the rate of increase in the general population of New England, it will be well to note what period of time was covered by these five generations. This we tabulate as follows:

TABLE I

Generation	Individuals in each Generation	Equivalent Number of Pure-blooded Individuals	Eldest born	Youngest born	Percentage of Childless Marriages
I	2	2	1615(?)		0
II	7	7	1640	1660	0
III	49	24.5	1661	1707	2.7
IV	230	57.5	1680	1754	3.5
V	993	128.25	1705	1792	Unknown

The extent to which the generations overlapped each other will be apparent at a glance. It is customary, in checking the chronology of a long line of descent, to allow 100 years for 3 generations, or an average of 33-1/3 years to a generation. In lines of descent tracing through the Thomas family the average length of a generation was somewhat under 30 years, or considerably below the supposed average. The same observation may be applied to all the early New England families; for the rapidity with which generations succeeded one another was due to the early marriages which prevailed in Colonial days and to the fact that a larger number of children were produced during the first than during the second decade of wedlock.

It will be remembered that John Thomas came to New England

---

* Two of these were cousins, hence there were but five childless marriages.

shortly before 1640. In a table published in The New England Historical and Genealogical Register for October, 1922,* it is estimated
that the population of New England in 1640 was 25,000, and that by 1749
their progeny had increased to 400, 000. It is our intention to check
these figures by means of the known increase in the family of John
Thomas.

It obviously cannot be supposed that the 25,000 estimated inhabitants in the year 1640 were all, like John Thomas and his wife, young
adults just about to found a family. These figures include the children
already born in this country, many children recently brought here by
their parents, and some adults above the usual age of parenthood, as
well as the young adults in whom we are interested. But inasmuch as
the years 1630 to 1640 had witnessed a tremendous influx of settlers,
and since a large proportion of these settlers are known to have been
young adults, it is fair to assume that the ratio of adults between 20
and 40 years of age was very much higher than is the case in a nor-
mally balanced population. Let us assume, then, that there were
10,000 young adults who already were, or were soon to become, heads
of families; this leaves 15,000, made up of the many children already
born to the above adults, adults above the usual age of parenthood,
adults who died in this country without issue, and adults who returned
to England with their families subsequent to 1640. The last two classes
were somewhat larger than is generally supposed. The question then
is: What would be the progeny of these 10, 000 heads of families by
the year 1748, on the basis of the increase in the family of John
Thomas? The following table shows the number of descendants of
John Thomas who were living in 1748:

TABLE II

Generation	Indivduals living in 1748		Equivalent Number of Pure-blooded Individuals
III	17	÷ 4	$4 \frac{4}{16}$
IV	59	÷ 8	$7 \frac{6}{16}$
V	471	÷ 16	$29 \frac{7}{16}$
VI	92	÷ 32	$2 \frac{14}{16}$
Totals	639		$43 \frac{15}{16}$

The figures for the third and fourth generations are those of individuals who survived until 1748; of the fifth generation 557 individuals had been born, of whom 86 had died, leaving 471; and a few had
been born in the sixth generation. In 1748 there were 639 known descendants of John Thomas living, and there were in addition, presumably, a few more, who have not been traced. But these 639 in-

* Vol. 76, p. 306, in an article by Rufus Stickney Tucker, Ph. D., entitled
"The Expansion of New England."

dividuals represent not merely the progeny of John Thomas but also, through intermarriage, a part of the progeny of other ancestors. It is therefore necessary to reduce the individuals in each generation to the equivalent number of pure-blooded individuals. Descendants in the third generation, for instance, represent 4 grandparents, and their number must be divided by 4; those in the fourth generation represent 8 great-grandparents, and their number must be divided by 8; and so with the other generations. On this basis we learn that by January, 1748/9, John Thomas individually was responsible for an increase of so close to 44 in the population that, since a few of his descendants are unlocated, we feel safe in calling the number 44 persons.

Now if each of our presumed 10,000 young adults was as prolific as John Thomas, they would be represented on January 1st, 1748/9 by 440,000 descendants. In Dr. Tucker's table alluded to above, these descendants are estimated at 400,000. In selecting the Thomas family for a test, one point was overlooked. Although John Thomas had but 7 children, which is close to the average for the second generation in New England, and under the average of children born, these 7 Thomas children all survived and had families, and this may have brought our 440,000 total too high. On the other hand, additional immigrants arrived after 1640 whose descendants helped somewhat to swell the total, and furthermore, as early as 1749, New England settlers had numerous descendants in New Jersey and on Long Island, and some descendants in other parts of New York and even in the south. We may conclude that Dr. Tucker's estimate, if it errs at all, errs on the side of conservatism.

Greatly differing estimates have been made of the total number of descendants whom each of the early Colonial settlers may claim, but most of these estimates are probably far below the actual figures. First, let us make an estimate based on the assumption that for seven generations succeeding the immigrant ancestor the rate of increase was 5 surviving children in each generation. Mr. J. Gardner Bartlett,* from an examination of 10,000 families, found about 6 surviving children in New England families between 1650 and 1845. Hence an estimate of 5 surviving children is very conservative, and it gives us 78,125 individuals in the eight generations. If we add the members of the intervening generations, and make allowance for those of the ninth, tenth, and even eleventh and twelfth generations who are already in existence, the total number of descendants of any one colonist of the period from 1620 to 1640 may well amount to over 200,000.

Lest this estimate be assailed as far above the fact, let us check it by some actual figures which fortunately are available. "The Munson Record," published at New Haven in 1895 and comprising 1,235 pages, had long held repute as a family history scarcely excelled for accuracy and completeness. The first index, 26 pages in length and containing only descendants of the Munson name, lists 4,671 individuals. Of these, 1,394, by actual count, were of the eighth generation.

* Journal of Heredity, vol. 10, p. 142.

Now it is generally known, — but the matter will be explained at length in the next paragraph, — that the descendants on female lines outnumber the name-bearing descendants by a ratio increasing with each generation. In the eighth generation the ratio is 126 descendants in female lines to every 2 (1 male and 1 female) born bearing the name. Hence the total number of descendants of Capt. Thomas Munson in the eighth generation may be estimated fairly closely as 64 x 1,394, i. e., 89,216. It will be seen that these figures are considerably above those arrived at from our original estimate made above; and, since Capt. Thomas Munson, of the first generation, had but one son and two daughters, it can scarcely be claimed that the example is an unfair one or one likely to lead to an overestimate.

An incidental study can be made from the tables of the Thomas pedigree which may be of interest to the writers of family histories. Too often publications of this sort are filled with descendants through female lines, to the neglect of the male lines. The chief objection to this practice, from a genealogical point of view, is the fact that a large proportion of the errors in such books occur in following the descendants of daughters, when the compiler treats of families with which he lacks familiarity. But there is also a statistical objection: the descendants through daughters, as has often been observed, multiply much more rapidly than descendants in the male line.

The sexes being about equally divided, let us suppose that John Doe has one son and one daughter, who in their turn have each likewise one son and one daughter. The grandchildren of John Doe, therefore, comprise one Doe grandson, a Doe granddaughter who will change her name on marriage, and two grandchildren born with a different name. That is, the ratio in the third generation is one male Doe to three who are females or of female descent. In the fourth generation the proportion will be 1 to 7, in the fifth generation 1 to 15, and in the ninth generation 1 to 255. Consequently, if a whole volume is required to set forth the male descendants of the Doe name, it will require 255 volumes to set forth the female lines in as adequate a manner. It need scarcely be added that no family history, no matter what its pretensions, has ever been published which treats at all completely of the female lines.

The theoretical ratio of increase as stated above may be tested by the actual figures of the descendants of John Thomas:

TABLE III

Generation	Descendants of the Thomas name	Females and Descendants through females	Theoretical Ratio
II	4	3	1 to 1
III	15	34	1 to 3
IV	30	200	1 to 7
V	61	932	1 to 15

It will be seen that the actual ratio between the male and female descendants is reasonably close to the theoretical ratio.

It is hardly necessary to point out that anyone desiring to make a similar test with some other family ought to select a family where the second generation was fairly evenly divided as to sex, for a great preponderance of either sex in the second generation is likely to affect the ratio for several subsequent generations. In later generations an occasional preponderance of boys or girls in certain families will not cause much variation from the theoretical ratio, since the total numbers are large and exceptional families of one sex are likely to be offset by exceptional families of the other.

Another interesting study is the geographical distribution of the Thomas descendants of the fifth generation. It has been mentioned that one reason for selecting this family for study was the fact that the children and grandchildren remained near the place of their nativity. It is, therefore, somewhat surprising to find that the great-great-grandchildren were distributed through 57 towns in Connecticut, 18 towns in New York, 8 towns in Massachusetts, 8 towns in Vermont, 3 towns in Pennsylvania, 1 town in New Hampshire, 1 town in Ohio, and 1 town in New Brunswick. These residences were the places of death, when known; otherwise the last known places of residence. If the place of death could have been found in all instances, the number of residences in New York, Ohio, and the west, would doubtless have been increased.

> *Oft did the harvest to their sickle yield;*
> *Their furrow oft the stubborn glebe has broke;*
> *How jocund did they drive their team afield!*
> *How bowed the woods beneath their sturdy stroke.*
> *—Thomas Gray.*

XVI
GENEALOGY AND EUGENICS

Examine well your blood.—Shakespeare.

In a psychological point of view it is, perhaps, questionable whether from birth and genealogy, how closely scrutinized soever, much insight is to be gained.—Carlyle.

Genealogy stands midway between the law and the biological sciences, and its relation to the latter is vital and far-reaching. Eugenics, in particular, is dependent on genealogy for much of its data. In breeding dogs and horses, each individual is registered, and the pedigrees are preserved. We have been less particular with regard to human mating. This is evidenced by the statistics of crime, of imbecility, and even of divorce. Genealogy has to depend on records much less complete, and human pedigrees have to be worked out, often at considerable labor and expense, from public records which, from the genealogical point of view, are at times sadly defective.

Undeniably, the studies made by eugenical students are of high potential value, looking to the betterment of social conditions in coming generations. At the present time it is possible that theories have run somewhat ahead of the established body of eugenical fact. No science gains by an attitude of dogmatism, and it is too early for a youthful science, such as eugenics, to assume such an attitude. The chief need of the present is research, to build up a larger body of proved fact, from which unassailable conclusions may be deduced.

A large number of the errors of fact to be found in some books written by eugenicists are attributable to lack of knowledge in handling genealogical books, and to the placing of too much confidence in the statements of these works. A few words of caution will therefore be apropos.

Many family histories have been produced by enthusiastic novices, whose enthusiasm is too often the only qualification they bring to the task. The man who would seek the advice or services of a trained expert in any other field of human activity, considers himself quite competent to compile a history of his family. Without previous experience, without knowledge of record sources of information, and often without the kind of mentality capable of handling and arranging the infinite detail of facts, names and dates, it is small wonder that his book, more often than not, is a hodge-podge of traditional statements, guesses, and misinterpreted and misplaced records, interspersed with actual proved facts. Occasionally, results are not much better when an incompetent professional is employed. The expert genealogist can tell after brief examination whether a genealogical book appears to be reasonably trustworthy. Naturally, the eugenicist, whose training lies in other directions, does not so readily detect the unreliability of many family histories.

Again, when an expert genealogist is employed to do the research, or at least the compiling or editing of such a book, he is bound by the ideas or instructions of his employer. While the resultant book gains in accuracy, it is still not entirely suited to the requirements of the eugenicist, since the financial backer of the book usually prefers to omit any facts which the family might consider discreditable.

Such defects in the genealogical source material have influenced some eugenical opinions which may not be ratified when a larger and more accurate body of fact is available.

For example, the earlier family historians were "sold" on the idea that most of the colonial families derived, whether immediately or remotely, from the English gentry. More recent investigations have demonstrated that they came very largely from the middle and lower classes. The notion has survived, however, in a somewhat altered form, to the effect that the first settlers were a specially selected group. Eugenicists have expressed the opinion that "pioneering" stock must have been, in the main, fundamentally sound stock.

It is not my intention to dispute this thesis. It may, however, be mentioned that many cases of lameness, defective eyesight, and other physical defects, are referred to in records of the first settlers. Also, that a physician's journal of about 1650 proves that he treated sporadic cases of gonorrhea. Six cases of sodomy are found among the immigrant founders of a single colony. Many, apparently sound themselves, carried neurotic strains which "came out" in the second American generation. So many exceptions of various types may be noted that, in the absence of authoritative statistics, it is unwise to assert the extent to which the first settlers constituted a "sound stock." Certain it is that this original homogeneous stock, marrying almost entirely within itself, produced in some localities within a few generations a notably fine crop of imbeciles and other defectives.

A single example will illustrate the difficulty, even the danger, of arriving too quickly at positive conclusions. Among the early New England colonists was Mr. William Tuttle, a gentleman who belonged to the small minority which really can be traced to the lesser gentry of England. His personal record seems to have been excellent. He and his wife had twelve children, all of whom lived to maturity, and ten of whom had issue. Truly, a prolific stock, and we may suppose of hardy physical constitution. In the second generation, however, violent temper manifested itself, amounting at times to dementia. The son David was incompetent, never married, and died at the age of fifty-four. The daughter Mercy suffered from periodic dementia, and in one fit killed one of her own children. The daughter Elizabeth was with child by another man when she married; was subsequently unfaithful; and the records of her divorce indicate quite clearly that she too suffered from periodic dementia. Finally, the son Benjamin, following a quarrel with his sister Sarah, who also had a violent temper, went outside and later returned with an axe, with which he killed her by a blow on the head.

Of later cases of insanity in this family, we will mention only a great-grandson Moses, whose father's will referred to him as "distracted" the same year that he was tried for a crime of violence; a great-great-grandson Elisha, who was "demented" but apparently harmless; and Thirza, whose story is specially remarkable, because it follows so closely the history of her remote uncle Benjamin. This unfortunate woman was descended from William Tuttle by three different lines, including one which affords other instances of insanity. In 1824, following a quarrel one Sunday morning between herself and her husband, he lay down and dozed; she went outside, came in with an axe, and killed him by a blow on the head. The family tradition is that she was psychotic and believed that her husband was trying to poison her.

Yet the descendants of William Tuttle, numbering probably over half a million, have contributed immeasurably to American culture in politics, religion, art, and industry. After ten generations, it is clear that nature has found this prolific family worthy to survive, and set upon it her stamp of approval. Doubtless the neurotic strain has been "bred out" of most branches. It is also a matter of interest that Elizabeth, one of the insane daughters of William Tuttle, became an ancestress of the illustrious Jonathan Edwards family, which has become almost a classic example of "good" heredity. In this branch, the energy and vigor of the early Tuttles was retained without the insanity, and union with the sane, shrewd normality of the Edwards family and the brilliance of the Stoddard connection, produced unusually happy results. Later marriages into families of mental ability have maintained the superior endowment of the descendants, although education and social environment may well have been factors in maintaining the superiority of the Edwards group.

No genealogist of long experience can remain blind to the part that heredity plays in human destiny. I have concluded from my own studies that in the long run nature eliminates the most degenerate human strains. But this is a slow process, and in its course entails not only suffering on the part of defectives, but also, if the defectives are vicious or led into crime, on the part of those who may be their victims.

By learning how nature works, and by utilizing human reason in the deliberate application of natural laws, the process of elimination of the unfit can be hastened, and needless suffering reduced to a minimum. Experience with plant and animal breeding proves that the program of eugenics is definitely within the realm of the possible. The kindest way to eliminate the unfit, and thus raise the average of human efficiency, is to prevent the reproduction of the unfit when the family history clearly indicates that most of the progeny are almost certain to be defective.

It does not fall within the province of this chapter to discuss how eugenic principles may be applied in a practical way and without antagonizing popular prejudice. The thing of first importance is to make absolutely sure of the laws governing human heredity. They are highly complicated; and the danger is that the traits which make us healthy animals may possibly conflict with other traits which make us intelligent and moral men and women. There may be the risk that in eliminating an undesirable trait, a desirable trait linked with it may also be "bred out."

Therefore it behooves the eugenicists to make sure of all the factors that have to be considered, before inaugurating too comprehensive or revolutionary a program. At present, the segregation of palpable defectives can be undertaken, both for their own protection and happiness, and with the object of keeping them from reproducing their kind. Research should continue, and in this genealogy must play a part. But it will have to be a eugenicized type of genealogy. Even the most expert genealogists today are not in a position to collect the kind of data concerning physical and mental traits that the science of eugenics requires. Obviously, the amateur will collect only what interests himself, while the professional will be limited by the wishes of his client. The only solution is for eugenics to develop its own genealogists, trained not only in eugenical principles and methods but also in genealogical methods of research. In the past, eugenics has indeed tried, with some success, the experiment of training its own "field workers," but naturally the stress has been on the eugenical side of the training. Those who have given such courses of training have been eugenicists, themselves not trained in genealogical research.

If even a dozen persons of the required mental aptitude could be trained in both eugenical and genealogical methods, and funds raised to set them to work for a period of from three to five years in several small old towns, one searcher to a town, collecting the proper kind of data both from descendants and from record sources, a body of unassailable fact concerning the families of these separate towns would be built up from which more than tentative conclusions might be drawn. Much excellent work has been done in the study of specific families of various types. But in my own genealogical work I have found too many things that do not seem to be adequately explained by eugenical theories; one branch of an unusually "poor" family rising to ability and prominence; or an exceptionally able family which after successive "good" marriages has produced undesirable individual members or has "gone to the dogs" in whole branches. Ability is so often found linked with mental or physical disorders that this phase of the study merits a large amount of research. Let the research continue, and while awaiting more positive data, arouse public interest in a subject the importance of which to the human race is second to none.

A pious disposition is certainly inherited.—Galton.

XVII

GENEALOGY AND THE LAW

Along about the middle of the nineteenth century it was, in the average country town, nobody's business, except the parents', when a child was born. . . . . . The Nomad could give the name of one New Englander, of the eighth generation born in New England, the passport statement of whose birth rests upon an assurance by his older sister that she remembered him at home as a little boy.
—*"The Nomad"* in the Boston Evening Transcript, 1930.

Scientific genealogy is closely allied to the law. The genealogist, if he is to make correct deductions from his source material, must acquire no small knowledge of probate laws of inheritance and the laws relative to real estate which governed such matters in colonial days in the colony or province where he works on the records. Without this knowledge, I have known genealogists to fail to solve specific problems when the solution was quite apparent if they had had this knowledge to guide them.

On the other hand, the lawyer sometimes requisitions the services of the genealogist when a determination of the identity of heirs at law to an intestate estate is sought. Sometimes no little research is required to locate the heirs, and the special training of the genealogist fits him for the task.

In working for an attorney, the genealogist should be careful not to infringe on the legal side of the problem. If he interviews people who may be heirs to the estate, it is not his place to tell them definitely that they are heirs, or to inform them of the size of the estate or what their proportion is likely to be. There are sometimes queer quirks in the law of which the genealogist may not be cognizant, and he may embarrass the lawyer if he unintentionally misleads an heir. Again, it is advisable to give as little information as possible to those who may be heirs until every particle of information which they can give has been obtained; for where the inheritance of property is involved, it is not always certain that claims made are bona fide, and by talking too much the genealogist may really be giving impostors help in their misrepresentations.

To show how far back a genealogist may have to go in legal work of this kind, an example from my own experience may be of interest. A woman died in 1925 at the age of ninety-three, leaving considerable property. Her nearest known heirs were cousins, younger than herself, on the maternal side. No relatives were known on the paternal side, and it was believed that none was living. The law required, however, that diligent search be made, and the attorney who was administrator of the estate employed me to make a search. The woman's father was born in a different town, and the gravestone gave the place and his exact date of birth. Going there, I found that his birth was not recorded, but his baptism was found in church records six weeks after the birth date given on his stone. He was born in 1797, and was one of the younger children in a family of eleven, the eldest of whom was born in 1779.

All of these eleven were uncles and aunts of the woman who left the estate, and each one of them had to be traced to determine whether they left children who would as first cousins of the decedent share in the inheritance. The youngest uncle settled in New York City, and by a careful search of New York directories over a period of eighty years, the address of a granddaughter was found. I interviewed her and got addresses of relatives. Thus slowly, step by step, the heirs were traced. No living first cousins were found on the paternal side to share in the bulk of the property, which by Connecticut law went to surviving first cousins. But realty in New York was inherited under the laws of that State by the heirs of deceased first cousins per stirpes, and for that part of the property upwards of sixty heirs were located on the paternal side.

Once I was employed by a firm of lawyers on a very different kind of case. An elderly American woman who had married an Englishman returned to this country and desired to resume American citizenship. The difficulty was that she was born in France while her father, a New York banker, was sojourning there, and her birth certificate, which had been obtained, failed to specify that her father was an American citizen. It was essential to prove that he was and the lawyers had tried several methods to establish it, including an unsuccessful attempt to secure a record of the father's passports from the proper government agency. So I was asked to see what I could do.

Ascertaining that the father died in New York on a certain date, I sent there for a photostatic copy of his death certificate. That gave the names of his parents and stated that he was born in Albany, N. Y., in 1842. However, I questioned whether this alone would be sufficient. This was not a federal document; and the statements made on it were not made by the man himself, nor under oath, and presumably were based on information given by his family just after his death.

So I asked my Washington agent to obtain photostatic copies of records of the family in the 1850 Census of Albany and in the 1870 Census of New York City. The former showed the man (with age correctly stated as 8), with parents of the same names as those which appeared on his death certificate, and birthplace stated as New York State. The 1870 Census showed him as a banker, aged 28, not yet married, but with a woman living with him whose name and age corresponded with those of his mother in the Albany Census of 1850. Why did I ask for the 1870 Census? That, I knew, was the first census which had two columns at the extreme right headed "citizen" and "alien"; and after the banker's name the "citizen" column was checked.

These census records are federal documents. The statements on them dovetailed with the man's death certificate. Taken together, the three pieces of evidence had to convince the government that the woman's father was a citizen, and so the case was happily closed.

Often there is more of human interest in estate work than in the tracing of ancestors who are all dead. Many years ago, I handled a case of this sort, and it makes a pretty story. A small estate was involved and the heirs were all known except for an aunt who went with her husband to California at the time of the Gold Rush. If this aunt had children still living, they would be entitled to share in the estate.

It was known by the eastern heirs that she had two children, whom we may call Adelaide and Charles, but nothing had been heard from them since the 1860's. After considerable searching of census records and pension files, Charles was at last located, still alive, in a Soldiers' Home in California. Here, we thought, our troubles had ended; but Charles wrote us that in 1873 his sister Adelaide had married a man named, let us say, Black, and had moved to another county. Since then, he had lost all track of her.

So the search had to begin again. Through census records we learned the names of four children of the Blacks and then advertised for them in a California newspaper. The item was called to the attention of Miss Black, one of Adelaide's children, and she write us that her mother was not living. She owned the family Bible which had belonged to her mother and grandmother, and it contained the entire family record, which she copied for us. Adelaide had written of her brother Charles: "supposed lost at sea, 1873"; and had died without knowing he was still living. I gave Miss Black the address of her uncle Charles, as she wished to correspond with him and seemed very much pleased to learn she had an uncle living.

A year later she wrote me that she had paid him a visit. He was delighted to see her and enjoyed her visit immensely. It was over fifty years since he had seen a relative; and he reproached himself bitterly for having lost touch with his sister and her family. Miss Black invited him to her home for a return visit, and he was happily looking forward to it. He died very suddenly the evening before he had planned to leave. Miss Black wrote me of the satisfaction she felt in having met and visited with him before it was too late.

Except for a will carelessly drawn by a woman living at the other end of the continent, which left part of her property intestate and made it necessary to search for the heirs at law, this meeting of uncle and niece on the Pacific coast would never have occurred. Little incidents like this break the monotony of the genealogist's work, and freshen and vitalize it with the warm pulse of human life.

What I possess, I see far distant lying;
And what I lost, grows real and undying.
—Unknown.

XVIII
DATES AND THE CALENDAR

Names, dates and places are the working material of the genealogist, and for ease and accuracy in handling dates the genealogist should possess or develop a mathematical ability. He should realize at a glance that a man born in 1738 was too young to marry in 1751; and that he probably did not marry a woman born in 1724. Experience teaches him to weigh problems of date and to draw conclusions from them almost instantaneously.

When very few positive dates are available, and one desires to check the probability of an alleged pedigree or a series of relationships, it is helpful to assign "guessed" dates of birth. If the children of given parents are known from probate or other records, but their birth dates are not found recorded, these can often be guessed from known dates. If the age of one of the children is stated in a death, pension or other record, then for this one we have an approximate date of birth, usually not more than a year wrong in either direction. We may then enter the birth date of this child, preceded by the word "circa" — Latin meaning "about" — or its abbreviation, "c." or "ca."

From what is known, we can work towards the unknown, and group the other children about the one to whom an approximate date of birth has been assigned. The marriage dates of some of the children may be known, and birth dates may be guessed from these, on the basis that a boy usually married at from 22 to 26, and a girl at from 18 to 23. When one of the girls had recorded children born from 1721 to 1745, for example, then at a glance we can set down 1700-1701 almost with certainty as close to her actual date of birth. For those children whose birth dates are merely guessed from their dates of marriage or from other circumstances such as when a youth was made a freeman or first began dealing in land, the fact that the birth date is hypothetical should always be indicated by placing it in brackets or parentheses, as for example, "(say 1703)."

When we have arrived at such approximate dates for the births of all the children, the advantage is the picture it gives us of the family as a whole. Suppose our problem is the parentage of one Charles Evans, who, we had theorized, might belong to the family group whose approximate ages we have been working out. Suppose we know, from his age at death, that he was born about 1685. The births of the children we have worked out can be placed with extreme probability between 1698 and 1715. In that case it seems more likely that our Charles, born about 1685, belonged to the previous generation, possibly an uncle of the children with the guessed dates of birth, or possibly of a different family entirely.

For many reasons it is advantageous in doing research to consider the entire family group, not to look upon each ancestor as an isolated individual, or as a mere link in a chain of descent. One of the most important reasons is that it enables us to check the chronology. Very often, the relations of dates determine or negate the possibility of an alleged line of descent, or provide clues which might otherwise elude detection. It is a good idea, while working, to write out the full family history, or chart the relationships, including the "guessed" dates when positive dates are not known. It is a great aid to the memory as well as to the imagination, if the eye can see the members of the family grouped together.

Another advantage sometimes accrues from working on the entire family group. If a brother or sister of our direct ancestor died in middle life or old age unmarried leaving any property, the probate of that collateral relative may provide important information; if there is a will, it will almost certainly name some of the relatives, and if not, the probate should list all the heirs at law. The best proof, sometimes the only proof, of our own line, may be missed if we consider only direct ancestors and neglect records of the collaterals.

There is one technical matter affecting dates which needs to be studied in some detail if the genealogist is to understand and properly interpret the Old Style and New Style dates. This is the important calendar change of 1752. As few things are more confusing to the inexperienced searcher, a complete explanation of it will be given.

The Julian calendar was used throughout the Middle Ages in Europe. Its inaccuracy amounted to about three days in every four centuries. By the time the Gregorian Calendar (named after Pope Gregory XIII) was promulgated in 1582, calendar dates were ahead of actual time by ten days. Since actual time is the time it takes the earth to make one complete revolution about the sun (a year), eventually the summer months would have come in winter and vice versa, if the calendar had been left uncorrected.

Roman Catholic countries adopted the Gregorian Calendar in or shortly after 1582. The Greek Church did not approve the calendar revision, and consequently Greece, Bulgaria and Russia were on the Old Style calendar until the time of the first World War, when they were thirteen days ahead of sun time. The conservatism of the English and the fact that the new calendar was sponsored by a Pope, delayed acceptance of it in Great Britain and the British colonies until after the passage of an Act of Parliament in 1751. By then the old calendar was eleven days ahead of sun time, so the Act provided that in 1752 the second day of September should be followed by the fourteenth day of September. In other words, what would have been September 3rd was called the 14th, exactly eleven days being thus dropped out of the year.

The cause of the error was the addition of a day to the calendar each fourth year (Leap Year). The dropping of the eleven days in 1752 brought the calendar back into fairly close harmony with sun time; and to provide against a recurrence of the trouble, it was also decided that on the even centuries no Leap Year day should be added except in a century divisible by 400. Thus 1800 and 1900 were not Leap Years, but the year 2000 will be.

The effect of the calendar change was to make every person born on or before 2 Sept. 1752 (and after 29 Feb. 1700) eleven days older (by the new calendar) than the record of his birth (Old Style) would indicate. A child born on 2 Sept. 1752 (the last day of the Old Style) would be, by the calendar, twelve days old on the following day, 14 Sept. 1752 (the first day of the New Style). It was natural that most of those living in the American colonies in 1752 should "rectify" their birth dates, setting them ahead by eleven days (to New Style). George Washington was born 11 Feb. 1731/2. Like most men of his generation, he rectified his birth date, making it 22 Feb. 1732. The latter is the date on which he would have been born if the New Style calendar had been in effect in 1732 — which it was not.

Parenthetically, it should be noted that those born on or before 29 Feb. 1700 needed to push their birth dates ahead ten days, not eleven, to change them to the New Style equivalent. The reason is that 1700 had a Leap Year day, which it would not have had under New Style, and that made up one of the eleven days lost by the calendar change in 1752. Not all of those living in 1752 understood this technicality and some no doubt incorrectly rectified their birth dates.

Although it was (and is) incorrect to change the dates prior to 14 Sept. 1752 into New Style, it was so generally done by those then living that the genealogist has to make allowance for it. Suppose, for example, that a group of brothers and sisters were born between the years 1743 and 1760. The older children were born before the calendar change, and in the town records the Old Style dates were therefore used in entering their births. The first child was born, let us say, 25 May 1743. Now, after all the children had been born, the parents bought a Bible and entered in it their own marriage and the births of the children, giving New Style dates for all the children, including those born before 1752 whose birth dates should properly have been entered Old Style. Consequently we find that the eldest child (whose birth in the town records had been contemporaneously entered as occuring 25 May 1743) appears in the Bible as born 5 June 1743. Both dates are correct, but the former is the date that ought to be used unless the latter has the words "New Style" added to show that it is a "rectified" date.

A further effect of the calendar change should be mentioned. When a man born between 29 Feb. 1700 and 2 Sept. 1752 died after 1752, and his age at death was stated exactly in years, months and days, the resultant date of birth (figured from age at death) is the New Style date of birth, and therefore eleven days later than the Old Style date in use at the time of birth. For example, Ephraim Burr, by his gravestone, died 29 Apr. 1776 aged 76 years and 13 days. Subtracting the age gives us 16 Apr. 1700 for his birth, but of course to get the Old Style date then in use we must subtract eleven days more. His birth was not recorded, but he was baptized 14 Apr. 1700, two days before his New Style date of birth. After subtracting the eleven days, we find that his real date of birth, by the Old Style calendar then in use, was 5 Apr. 1700, which was nine days before he was baptized. Obviously, he could not have been baptized two days before he was born, which is the result we get if we fail to make allowance for the calendar change.

The general rule is: When a child was born before Sept. 1752 and the birth was recorded contemporaneously, add eleven days to the date to obtain the New Style equivalent; and when a person born prior to Sept. 1752 dies and a record states his exact age at death, subtract the age from the date of death, and then subtract eleven days more to obtain the Old Style equivalent. As already explained, for those born on or before 29 Feb. 1700, ten days instead of eleven should properly be used.

Exact ages were not always stated, and unless the days are specified, the presumption is that the age is not precise. When a record states that a man died aged fifty years and eight months, he may have been that age to a day, but he may have been a few days over the fifty years and eight months. Recorders and gravestones do not always specify the age to a day.

One other change was made in 1752, and that was the date beginning the New Year. The succession of seasons and years is an astronomical fact, caused by the orbit of the earth about the sun. But the selection of one day on which to start a new year is an artificial and arbitrary matter. Various peoples in various ages have celebrated different New Year's Days. Some of the ancient races ended their year with a harvest festival, and the Jews still start their new year at that season. Others began the year with the vernal equinox, when the earth in the northern hemisphere seems to renew its life. Easter came at that season, and the date used by Christians for New Year's Day was quite generally March 25th, though in the early centuries some used the date December 25th, the traditional birthday of Christ.

The only dates in general use for New Year's Day among the English colonials were January 1st, the historic secular date, and March 25th which, as we have seen, was of religious significance and was usually employed in church registers. The Act of Parliament in 1751 established January 1st as New Year's Day for 1752 and subsequent years, and thereafter we are relieved of the confusion resulting from two possible dates of beginning the year. This change did not, like the dropping of eleven days, have any effect on the ages of persons then living. Some have misunderstood this and have supposed that it caused a difference of nearly three months in people's ages; such a misunderstanding may be found in the explanatory notes prefaced to the Coolidge Genealogy (1930). When the names of the months of birth were entered, such a notion is unthinkable.

Before 1700 and in some later records, recorders sometimes used the number of the month instead of the name. This was usually the practice of the Quakers. Of course, March was then numbered as the first month, since New Year's Day fell in it, and dates before March 25th as well as those succeeding it were reckoned as falling in the first month. April was the second month, and May the third. The early Quaker records were often very precise, stating that an event occurred on "the 10th of the 5th month which is called July." When the number of the month was stated in any record prior to 1752, the genealogist should reckon March as the first month and February as the twelfth.

If a record states that John Jones was born on the 10th of the fifth month, 1710, this must be Old Style and means that he was born in July. After 1752, July became the seventh instead of the fifth month, but that does not affect the fact that John Jones was born in July. However, if he was born after July 20th, the eleven-day change in 1752 would push his birth date into early August, if "rectified" to the New Style date.

Before 1752, there is likely to be some confusion with regard to dates between 1 January and 24 March, unless we know what New Year's Day a particular recorder used. It is apparent that if the year began 25 March, a man born on 20 February was born before the new year began, hence a year earlier than if the year began 1 January. If 1710 began on 25 March, then a man born on 20 February following was born in 1710, since 1711 did not begin until the next month. The only problem in this connection is the year in which dates between 1 January and 24 March should be placed, and we always run the chance of an error of exactly a year if we do not know the date on which the recorder began the New Year. In most records before 1700 we may usually assume that the year was reckoned as beginning March 25th, and that is true of many later records, especially church registers. But the use of 1 January gradually came into favor, especially in legal documents and town records, even before that date was made official in 1752. Careful recorders often used a double date, such as 11 Feb. 1731/2; here we can be sure that the year is 1732 by modern usage, but the double date should be retained when records are copied and printed. Savage and some other early genealogists modernized all year dates, but it is better practice to retain the year date as given in a record, and far safer if it is a double date.

Some early records give an erroneous impression because of the uncertainty as to when the recorder started his year. In the vital records of Norwich, Conn., we read that Robert Wade married 11 Mar. 1691, and that his first child was born Jan. 1691. We may assume that the marriage occurred 11 Mar. 1690/1 and that the recorder used the later year date because he was thinking of March as the first month of the new year. The child was born Jan. 1691/2, ten months later, but it was still 1691 until the new year began in March. Remember that this confusion, before 1752, of year dates applies only to dates between 1 January and 24 March, since all other dates belong to the same year regardless of when New Year's Day was celebrated.

XIX
HOW TO TRACE YOUR ANCESTRY

Start two files. The first should be "Source Material" and will contain all the information you receive or obtain from relatives, printed works and public records. Use some system of numbering these items so that they can be readily located when you need to check with them. The second file should be your arranged material on your various family lines. Here you will bring together the information obtained from all sources, so far as you consider it trustworthy, and what you enter here should be keyed by reference numbers to the papers in the "Source Material" file. Thus, when you need to check the arranged material or "Genealogy" and to add to it or correct it, you can readily find the sources of your statements. For this arranged material, some find that it helps to use one of the several forms which are on the market. Others find it easier to organize the Genealogy without the aid of printed forms.

The first data in your Source Material should be what you know of your own personal knowledge, and then all the information you can possibly obtain from the older members of your family and from collateral relatives. Some of them may possess a Bible or family record pertaining to one of your lines. Ask the relatives for names not only of parents, grandparents and others in the direct line, but for the brothers and sisters so far as known in each generation. Even the names of collateral relatives are sometimes important as clues because family names were often transmitted from the earlier to the later generations. Ask for the residences of all these people and, when known, places and dates of birth, marriage and death. If a near ancestor died this side of 1900 (and in some states considerably earlier than that), you can write to the custodian of such records (whether registrar, town clerk or board of health) for his death certificate which, if you are lucky, may state his date and place of birth and even the names of his parents.

Several textbooks are availabe which list sources. To find where official vital statistics are kept in each state, one of the best I know is Noel C. Stevenson, Search and Research, revised edition 1959, Deseret Book Co., Salt Lake City, Utah.

During the period between the Revolution and 1850 or even later, when vital statistics were kept poorly if at all in most parts of the country, a newspaper obituary is often a godsend. If the older members of your family preserved clippings, obtain or copy them. If not, you may have to learn what city or county newspaper was published at the time and in the locality where your progenitor died. Clarence S. Brigham, History and Bibliography of American Newspapers 1690-1820 (2 vols., 1947), and Winifred Gregory (ed.), American Newspapers 1821-1936, will usually direct you to those libraries where specific newspaper files may be consulted. You will have to write to the library, and perhaps pay someone, to look for and copy the desired items.

If a grandfather, or even a great-uncle, was a Civil War pensioner, by all means have his pension file consulted in the National Archives in Washington. These files sometimes contain an amazing amount of family data, especially if the pensioner lived beyond 1900, when government forms asked for considerable family information. It need hardly be added that if any of your ancestors served in the War of 1812 or in the Revolutionary War — or in any of our national wars, their pension files should also be examined and abstracted. It sometimes pays to get an experienced genealogist in Washington to do this, for I have known of interesting and sometimes important data to be overlooked in official reports to inquirers which are supplied for a trivial sum.

The United States census schedules are another invaluable aid. Starting in 1850, they give the name, age and state of birth of all members of each household. If you had a grandsire born a little earlier than 1850, and know the locality, you should find him listed in the 1850 Census with his parents and sibs, and thus learn the names of his father and mother and the states in which they were born. Do not feel upset if inconsistencies or errors are occasionally encountered. If you obtain a listing of the family in both 1850 and 1860, you may find that your granny's age increased less than ten years during the decade, for that is a woman's privilege. Many of the schedules are remarkably accurate, but some of the enumerators were not men of much education or acumen, and it happened at times that the enumerator failed to find at home the member of the family best qualified to give information.

In 1880 the schedules give the state of birth not only for each person listed, but also that of each one's parents. So you thus get your ancestor's statement as to where his parents were born, although their names are not given. If your ancestor was then 70 or 80, you thus learn in what state to seek for records of the previous generation, who may have been born in the 1770's. Such information is usually accurate, and in any case helpful. Many of these schedules are now available (for their own states at least) at the state libraries or in the state archives, wherever kept, at least in copy or on microfilm. If necessary, a professional genealogist in Washington, D. C., can be employed to search them in the National Archives. Do not overlook other census records. For example, the state census taken in New York in 1855, 1865, etc., give more complete information than is found in the federal census of 1850, 1860, etc. The State Library in Albany, N. Y., can inform you as to how far these schedules have been preserved for each county and where they may be consulted.

You should now have much preliminary information in your Source Material file, the reference for each item being carefully entered there. It is time now to spend a few days or a week in a large genealogical library. You may perhaps find a printed family history dealing with one or more of the families in which you are interested, and sometimes you can easily link your own data with the earlier generations given in the book. Copy what the book gives on your own line, with the author, title and date of the book noted, but remember that the information may not all be entirely correct. As explained in earlier chapters, some family histories were compiled by competent researchers, others by genealogically ignorant enthusiasts. The librarian may be able to tell you whether a specific book or its author has a generally good or poor reputation; but remember that the best of books are not perfect and that mistakes may occur.

The date of publication of the genealogy is important. For example, if it was published back in 1886, presumably the information on a family group which was born (say) between 1790 and 1886 was supplied by a member of that group who was then living from personal and family knowledge. Hence the information within such date limits is likely to be reasonably correct. That does not mean that you are safe in accepting the data on the early generations which the compiler had to dig out item by item from original records (or copy from previously printed sources) and combine into a connected pedigree. He may have done this well, but he may not; and so far as possible the earlier generations should be checked with and verified from original record sources. Some of the genealogies published years ago are quite good. Even so, during the last half-century or longer, records in many of the older sections of the country have been indexed and made more readily accessible, and the early compilers often overlooked records now easily obtainable which may add to or even correct what they published.

You may have to expand the library work into two or three weeks, for you cannot afford to overlook the many records of families and places which have been published in periodicals. To find these records, the indexes mentioned in an earlier chapter should serve as a guide. There are other indexes, to which the librarian may refer you. Some of the articles deal with families which have no printed genealogies, others correct or add to what has appeared in family histories. Do not fail to consult, especially for the earlier generations, the records of places which have appeared in magazines or as separate books. Some of these are useful to check the accuracy of the family histories you used, while others may add new items to your notes.

Town histories and county histories should be consulted for those areas in which your ancestors lived. Some contain genealogies which very greatly as to authenticity. The most pretentious sometimes turn out to be the most undependable. Unless the searcher has by now acquired the ability to appraise the nature and value of such books, he can only copy data with his fingers crossed. The chief value of the county histories published fifty to a hundred years ago lies in the biographical and genealogical data supplied by the people then living, usually correct for their immediate families and those of their parents and grandparents, but often unsafe to follow when tradition and supposition were relied on for the earlier data. The same caveat applies to the Virkus Compendium of American Genealogy and similar publications.

HOW TO TRACE YOUR ANCESTRY

The searcher has now collected a lot of information, from family
sources, from official records, and from books and periodicals. If by
now he feels sufficiently experienced, and if able to travel to the
places where his ancestors lived and visit the repositories where the
contemporary unpublished records are kept, he will find this type of
research the most interesting and rewarding of all. If, however, he
feels confused and has begun to question whether he is equipped with
a genealogical type of mind (few are conscious of the lack!), it might
be wise to turn over his collected material to an expert to check and
evaluate. The expert may be able to tell him that some of the material copied from books or periodicals is false, or that some of it is
suspicious and needs to be verified. Specific research in documentary
sources may be recommended, and then the question is how far he
may feel able or willing to go in the matter of cost.

Let us suppose, however, that you do have a genealogical type
of mind, and that you have the time and the monetary resources to
search the documentary sources personally. You may find some or
all of these: vital statistics, probate records, land records, both
county and superior court records, colony records (many of these are
in print), church registers, cemetery or sexton's records — and perhaps others. Unlike the pension and census records, these are more
or less local. In some states a large number of them have been
gathered (in original, copy, or microfilm) into a central repository,
such as a State Library; in other states, they remain more scattered.

There are several books which tell (more or less thoroughly)
where to locate the different kinds of records in different sections of
the country. Some of these were mentioned in an earlier chapter.
Some of these books also explain, or do their best to explain, how to
handle and interpret the records you find. I doubt that it does much
good for a beginner to read such a book straight through. There is
too much which is unfamiliar and the reader cannot absorb it all. I
have always held that one learns best by doing. When you encounter
something in the records which puzzles you, then look it up in the
guide books, and if the explanation is there, it will now mean something to you and you will remember it. Textbooks have their uses,
but no one can sit down and read a book and thereby become an ac-
complished genealogist.

You will pick up the essential special knowledge as you proceed.
The calendar change and its effects, and double dating, you do have
to sit down and learn. These were explained in the last chapter. The
meaning in earlier centuries of various terms, especially terms of
relationship; probate law and custom in the colony where your ancestors lived; nomenclature and the variant spelling of names; the use of
nicknames even in legal documents and church records (Patty for
Martha and a host of others); the use of variant forms of a name, or
even confusion of names, for the same individual (such as Augustus,
Augustin and Austin for the same man, Mehitable and Mable for the
same woman) — these are just a few of the things you have to learn as
you work. There is also the matter of script. Different styles were
used at different periods, and you should acquire familiarity with
them in order to read the documents correctly. When it comes to

117

early seventeenth century script, the differences from modern writing are so great that this is a study in itself. I have known first-class genealogists, even professional ones, who could not read that script with ease.

You have to learn to discriminate between different kinds of wills. Some were composed with great care and the testator specified that certain children had received their portions, in part or in whole, making it certain that all the children were named. Other early wills read as if they were carelessly composed or hastily drawn, perhaps when the testator was dying. Some were nuncupative (word of mouth). With that type of will, it is unsafe to assume that it necessarily named every child or heir. Without a will a man died intestate and the court ordered distribution to the heirs at law. Usually a distribution in the files names all the children. However, I have seen cases where the court order of distribution (in a record volume, not the files) states that certain specified children had received their portions in the life-time of the deceased and therefore orders distribution to the remaining children, with the result that the filed distribution does not name all the surviving children.

In most of the colonies and states, probate and land records were kept at the county seat. In Rhode Island, Connecticut and Vermont, each town kept its land records, and in Rhode Island the probate records as well, while Connecticut and Vermont established probate districts which often cover more than one town but less than the county. The earlier deeds are a gold mine for the genealogist. Your ancestor may have sold land with his wife which she inherited from her family, and the deed discloses her identity. That is most important when the marriage was not recorded. After a man's death, one of his children may have bought out the other heirs, or they may have joined in a sale to an outsider. Such deeds provide a picture of the family group when estates were not probated or when the probate record is deficient. Sometimes the heirs sold the inherited land in separate deeds to a neighbor. To find them all, you will have to try the grantee index for the purchases made by this neighbor, for of course sales made by daughters of your ancestor with their husbands will not be found under his family surname in the grantor index. In some places, the land indexes were compiled by amateurs and are at times incomplete and inaccurate.

One or two concluding pieces of advice may not be amiss. Use names, not numbers, for the months. As already explained in the preceding chapter, the numbers used for months were changed in 1752. Hence, if you use figures for months and the date is earlier than 1752, the reader has no way to know whether you are following a contemporary record in which the figure 1 would mean March, not January, or whether you have changed the recorded figure to conform with modern usage. It is best to place the day before the month, for example, 2 Apr. 1782, rather than Apr. 2, 1782. Besides saving a comma in every date you write, fewer inaccuracies in copying occur when the dates are so written.

You should now have a lot of your ancestral lines arranged, referenced to your file of Source Material so that you can readily locate the authority for the facts you have accepted. After all the records have been searched and studied, some problems remain unsolved, some missing wives are still missing, some conclusions are only tentative. Most human beings are not sufficiently skeptical. They desire certainty. They do not like to quit with an inconclusive conclusion, such as that John is a proved son of William who was twice married; but while quite probably he belonged to the second wife, that is unproved and possibly he was a son by the first wife. That means, you see, that we are prohibited from setting forth our ancestry through either of the wives. And, it must be confessed, we are all tormented by those blank spaces on the ancestral chart. Hence when the missing maiden surname of an ancestor's wife is found stated somewhere — anywhere — perhaps in a newspaper genealogical column, bingo! It is copied onto the chart. Unless full evidence for the wife's identity was set forth, rub it out again; it is probably wrong. Develop a healthy skepticism. Accept nothing unreservedly until proved.

APPENDIX

THE BOARD FOR CERTIFICATION OF GENEALOGISTS

By Milton Rubincam, Chairman

For many years there was a growing demand by libraries, archival institutions, and societies for a register of competent genealogists and genealogical record searchers. To meet this demand the Board for Certification of Genealogists was incorporated in Washington, D.C. in June 1964 for the purpose of formulating standards of genealogical research and the establishment of a register of persons who are deemed to be qualified for this type of work. The Board's Trustees include distinguished genealogists, historians, and archivists from all parts of the United States.

The functions of the Board are to receive applications for certification, to determine if the applicants are qualified to do research by an examination of their works, to issue certificates of approval to applicants found to be competent to engage in professional research, to maintain registers of genealogists and genealogical record searchers, and to make lists of genealogists and record searchers available to libraries, archival institutions, societies, and private individuals.

Successful applicants for the designation of Certified Genealogists are authorized to place the initials "C. G." after their names, and to use the appropriate insignia on their letterheads, while certified Genealogical Record Searchers are entitled to add the initials "G. R. S." after their names, and to use the appropriate insignia. For the present, the Board's policy is to certify genealogists who work only in the field of American genealogy. There is a greater demand for record searchers, and the Board does consider applications from foreign as well as American record searchers.

The Board's Information Sheet, application forms, and definitions of "Genealogist" and "Genealogical Record Searcher" may be obtained from The Executive Secretary, Board for Certification of Genealogists, 1307 New Hampshire Avenue, N.W., Washington, D.C. 20036.

120